BROWN ENOUGH

**True Stories About
Love, Violence,
the Student Loan Crisis,
Hollywood, Race,
Familia, and
Making It in America**

CHRISTOPHER RIVAS

Row House Publishing recognizes that the power of justice-centered storytelling isn't a phenomenon; it is essential for progress. We believe in equity and activism, and that books—and the culture around them—have the potential to transform the universal conversation around what it means to be human.

Part of honoring that conversation is protecting the intellectual property of authors. Reproducing any portion of this book (except for the use of short quotations for review purposes) without the expressed written permission of the copyright owner(s) is strictly prohibited. Submit all requests for usage to rights@rowhousepublishing.com.

Thank you for being an important part of the conversation and holding sacred the critical work of our authors.

Library of Congress Cataloging-in-Publication Data Available Upon Request

ISBN 978-1-955905-04-6 (HC)
ISBN 978-1-955905-10-7 (eBook)

Printed in the United States
Distributed by Simon & Schuster

Book Design by Pauline Neuwirth, Neuwirth & Associates Inc.

First edition
10 9 8 7 6 5 4 3 2 1

This book is dedicated to all the little Brown kids who need to

see themselves grander and more vibrant:

I see you. I hear you. We here . . .

"I have not been able to disown the light into which I was born and yet I have not wanted to reject the servitudes of this time either."

—ALBERT CAMUS

Contents

Acknowledgments

The weight of this seems intense. As if I could sum up my gratitude into a paragraph or a page or a book or a lifetime. I will do my best:

My family, especially my parents whose best parenting technique was to say "yes" more than "no," to encourage that I walk toward my desires safely, even though the outcome was unknown.

My friends who never judged me (for the most part) for often turning my life into a laboratory of self. The ones who have been open, honest, and intimate with me, maybe for a moment, for a day, for an hour, or for a year.

The countless number of incredible people who helped read, and reread, and listened to me read, and then read some more.

Nirmala for your generous talent and heart.

Roof Kiki, for being a safe place and a best friend.

The poets, storytellers, artists, movers, creators, disrupters, and collaborators who challenged, fought, moved, and lit fires in me.

The ladies at Row House for being more badass than the rest, and for having foresight and vision beyond the rest.

[ACKNOWLEDGMENTS]

My agent, team, and the guy at Ikigai for belief and support in this kid from Queens who's always asking questions, still figuring it out, often publicly, and often at the crack of dawn.

And everyone and everything else who allow the world to keep moving—*Namu Amida Butsu*—my life is the result and the effort of others. Thank you.

An Invitation

In this book, there is no three-step plan to help you better understand colorism, colonization, police violence, the student loan crisis, family, love, or making it in America. I am not a Oprah or Tony Robbins or even Ibram X. Kendi. This book will not make you rich, solve all your problems, find you a soulmate, or fix the world.

I am not an expert because I am Brown. I do not speak on behalf of all Brown people. That is impossible. If I carry any expertise, it is that of experience. My experience—I was born this way, in this body, and I have lived this life to the best of my abilities. I know what hurts me and what helps me. Sometimes I avoid what helps and do what hurts even when I know I shouldn't.

Honesty is what I can control, honest with the fact that I can deeply want things to change and, at the same time, be complacent in the actions that keep things the way they are. Honest with my confusion, anger, love, rage, disruption, hurt, lust, and contradictions. Honest about how important and good it feels to see oneself and to be seen. Honest about how I am just beginning to discover a space that I didn't even know existed until

Ta-Nehisi Coates, a person some academics have called our modern-day James Baldwin, told me in a room full of people that there was no space for my Brown body in the race conversation.

Who would I have been had I known about this space?

The next many years was me finding out. I didn't know which way was up, so, like any good person in crisis, I started blowing things up in my life. I broke up with a great girlfriend because she was white, and I wrote a *New York Times* article about it, which ended up going viral, I lashed out at a cop and got thrown in jail, I accidentally radicalized a young Indian student of mine, I started learning Spanish, I started a podcast, I turned down jobs, I burned a lot of bridges, I booked a spot on a network sitcom, and I wrote stories about all of it.

I was a baby learning to walk again, tripping and falling all the way across the room. And that's what this book is about. Good intentions, falling down, asking big questions, knocking things over, and confronting the truth. As James Baldwin declared in *Notes of a Native Son*, "I gave the world murderous power over me."

Yes—me too.

Yes—anything to be seen. To be liked. To "make it."

"I gave the world murderous power over me." Yes, I did.

No more. No longer chasing the carrot dangling from my forehead that I was told would be some answer to some dream that wasn't even mine. No longer accepting a story that denies me my space. A large diverse space that once did not contain me, you, us . . . A space that is actually what the global majority of the world is and looks like. Brown. Colorful. Diverse. There is nothing new here. I am not filling this space or claiming it as my own, but simply moving through it, or letting it move through me; even better—I'm letting it move me.

And now, right now, I invite you to allow yourself to be moved.

Moved to speak, to create rituals, to grieve, and to take action. Action for the health of the community, which is everyone under the gaze of whiteness, because someone needs to bring love, exposure, and vulnerability to our invisible world. Someone needs to turn the light on and say, "My culture-filled, melanin-vibrant sisters and brothers, anyone who has felt left out or like their voice or actions don't matter—they do matter! You matter." And you can take part in that process.

With all your shades, colors, wounds, scars, and tattoos. With all your varied melanin. With all your Brownness. With all your vibrant color and what-ever-ness. With all your stuff. With all your trauma, your joy, your celebration, your history. With all the shit that comes with it. With anything and everything you are, will you join me in this space?

There's no going back now. I'm on a mission to find self, maybe my-self, maybe a collective self, maybe that includes my Brown self, maybe I will not feel so vague, confused, and questioning about my Brown identity and where I stand or belong. Maybe I will move beyond the labels and tags, and I will find more space where I am free to actually be myself, not some perfect self. Space is the Buddhist version of God—space to me is peace and rest from needing to get it all right, and it feels like there is a lot to get right. I am on a mission to ask the questions and take the actions necessary to create more space that allows me to recognize and rest in this: my perfectly ordinary everyday beautiful Brown self.

Indigenous peoples believe that anything that restores balance is medicine. A good meal, medicine. Some tea, medicine. A hike with a friend, medicine. A nap, medicine. A good car dance, medicine. Young Brown boys and girls embracing their gorgeous melanin, casting spells of self-worth, medicine, because the scales are out of whack, and it's time to restore them.

Will you join me?

Not in It

"There are places I can't go, like outside my body."

—YANYI

My mother has Lyme disease. It's a bitch of disease, running the gamut from headaches to joint pain, fatigue, total body swelling, numbness, complete paralysis, depression, and maybe even death. The worst part is that for twenty years my mom never even knew she had it. Until one day, out of nowhere, she got a horrible headache and part of her face went completely numb and paralyzed. Not a single doctor knew what was happening. It wasn't a stroke; it wasn't neurological; it was completely unknown. Looking for answers, she saw specialist after specialist, took test after test, hooked up to machine after machine, blood sample after blood sample, until eventually we discovered that my mother has ("has" because it never goes away) Lyme disease. She had been bitten by an infected tick in the woods of the Catskills, New York, more than twenty years earlier and didn't even know it.

Imagine waking up every day thinking you know your life and having no idea that you are carrying something that can and will strike at any moment. Then, suddenly, it's here, and you don't know if this is the worst of it or the best of it, you don't know when or how it will continue to take effect, and you aren't sure why, but it's here.

My mother's disorder is not much different than the condition of living in my own skin. My mother navigated her disease with little understanding of how to manage the impact it had on her. Meanwhile, I was dealing with the consequences of not understanding my Brownness's impact on me. This is what it's like for a person of color born into a white supremacist system. You think you're doing okay, and then white supremacy strikes again. You can think you are free from it, healed from it, but it is always there, lying in wait. You can go quite a while without an incident or symptoms. Then, a big flare-up, and you realize you've been carrying something all along—this thing your parents couldn't quite explain or prepare you for (even though they tried) because they still have it, and because their parents had it, and their parents' parents had it. We're all dealing with this system called white supremacy, handed down to us at birth, which grows more severe over time.

Maybe, if you're lucky, as in my case, you begin to notice that others can see the system, that they can see what you previously couldn't. Like a giant boulder that I've been carrying blindly on my back is now dropped into my arms, and now I know the weight that I am carrying. Now it begins to become clear to me that, no, I am not like my heroes on TV, or the people on billboards and magazines, I am not in the conversation, and all the pretending won't make it so. No, we don't all play the same game. No, it's not fair.

My moment of awakening that made me realize, "Oh shit, something's up here," came the night that I saw Ta-Nehisi Coates speak at an intimate gathering at a library in downtown LA. To be completely honest, at the time, I'd never heard of him before. But a friend of mine insisted he was a big deal and that I had to be there, and so I was. Coates was speaking about race (as he does), and everybody was filled with "Oohs," and "Aahhs," and the occasional "Yes, yes, brother." And it was well-earned; it was intellectual church.

Coates spoke about Black and white, and then he spoke about Black and white, and then he spoke about Black and white. When it came time for questions, I really didn't want to say anything, but I felt like I needed to, like this was a big moment to get woke, to be enlightened by the man some have called our modern-day James Baldwin. So, I raised my hand, got selected, and I asked: "Black and white, that's all I hear, Black and white. As a Brown man, a Dominican, Colombian Afro-Latino in this world, where does that leave me in the conversation?"

Coates took a short breath and responded quicker than most people think, "Not in it."

"Not in it?" I asked.

"Not in it," he coolly replied.

The moderator snatched back my microphone, and they moved on to the next question, and I sat down like a child reprimanded for asking a stupid question with a simple and obvious answer: "Of course not in it. How did I not know that?"

What a curse to not exist, I thought. To be pushed to the boundaries and left out is exile. Exile was and is the ultimate punishment of the gods, or The God (if that's your thing), handed down to Adam and Eve in the very first chapter of one of the books of this thing we call life, and then handed down again to Cain just a few pages later. To *not be in it* is the curse among all curses. To be left somewhere in between was absolute hell—Sisyphus, forced to push a giant boulder up a hill for an eternity with the hope of it staying at the top, only to watch it roll down again and again. Tantalus, forever hungry and forever thirsty with food and drink just out of his reach. To *not be in it* is not far off from purgatory. It is a middle place with no actual home or end point with which to identify.

It's handed down in Greek tragedy after Greek tragedy. Handed down to Romeo, who says it so painfully when exiled from Vienna, exiled from Juliet, from his love:

Ha, banishment? Be merciful, say "death." For exile hath more terror in his look, much more than death. Do not say "banishment" . . . purgatory, torture, hell itself. Hence "banishèd" is banished from the world. And world's exile is death.

After the talk, I was supposed to go to dinner with some friends, but I figured I'd be a real downer, so I went home and stared at the ceiling instead, wondering: "Not in it, why am I not in it? Where am I? Where are the Brown bodies? Where are our stories and our voices? Where are my father and mother? Where are the people I love?" It was as if something I didn't even know I owned was stolen from me.

Pain flooded my body, the pain of not being seen. It hurt my pride, like he was telling me my life was worth less than his. I thought, "At least you get your place in the conversation." For a long time, I took what Coates said as an insult, until I softened enough to see it as an honest fact. I don't imagine he was saying that I shouldn't be in it, but rather that I am not in it because I haven't been allowed to be. My Brown identity was and often is not pertinent to this conversation in which whiteness and Blackness are seen as polar opposites and point to the extremes that determine how and whether people are valued.

As a child, I had this immense loneliness, this lack of voice, this need to fit in and be seen. Suddenly, it began to make sense— oh, that is why white bodies who never have to think about what they look like became and sometimes still are my measuring stick for beauty and self-worth. That is why I so desperately had a hunger to be something other than what I am, a hunger that seemed to never be filled; a Brown body in a Black/white world just trying to fit in, trying to be in it. Trying to be seen. That hunger started slowly, through the images, stories, politics, and media that told me my Brown body doesn't thrive like those of others. These stories attacking my ability to live in my own skin. As a child, I remember that burning feeling of self-hate as I looked in the mirror, hating my thick curly hair and big nose, and hating that I didn't look like a member of NSYNC or the Mickey Mouse Club. To be clear, white supremacy impacts all marginalized, BIPOC, multiheritage, global majority people, and not simply Brown folks. Its symptoms and how it manifests are different for everyone—its nuances, stresses, and dangers (internally and externally) are unique and also the same for many.

The next day at a friend's birthday party, I told one of my best friends, Affan, about what had happened with Ta-Nehisi the night before. Affan is a fellow Brown man from Pakistan, and I often go to him when I have to complain about cultural identity issues. I told Affan the story and, in his very nonchalant, everything is always super chill attitude, he asked, "Okay, so, what are you gonna do about it?"

Feeling challenged, I asked him right back: "Fuck you, that's you, too, what are you gonna do about it?"

"What did you expect him to say?" Affan asked. "He spoke his truth. You can go speak yours." And then he offered me a hit of the blunt he was smoking. I inhaled, and he went on, "We all gotta speak up for ourselves, because they [he meant white people] ain't gonna do it for us."

I exhaled, and it clicked, I am in charge of all the words I don't speak. I must speak. A mantra and a belief unearthed upon hearing those words *not in it*.

There is an African proverb that says, "Until the lion learns to write, every story will glorify the hunter." This is why I must write, so that others stop doing it for me. I will no longer be passive to a narrative that doesn't include my body. If I'm not in the existing conversation, I'm going to start a different conversation that claims my own Brown worth and my own Brown experience.

There are things that happen to me that fall into a very distinctive point on the timeline. There is a *before the moment* and *after the moment*. I can easily forget many of the details of life before the moment. Like snow melting in an instant. One morning it's there all piled up and then by afternoon, it's gone, because melting is a nonlinear process. Melting begets melting. The melting has probably been happening for weeks unseen, and then all of a sudden everything below the surface is hot enough to make it all change.

There was before this moment with Coates—snow.

And then there was after—water.

Something snapped in me, unlocked potential in me, I might find this voice, I might learn to fill that vast space. A glowing darkness, which was both exhilarating and daunting.

It's like in the TV show *Woke*—the lead character is a Black cartoonist on the verge of mainstream success, until he has an all-too-common encounter with an overly aggressive white policeman, and all of a sudden, our hero starts to see and hear inanimate objects talking to him. Everything is alive and awake with race and its nuances, and all the everyday microaggressions he'd tried to ignore before, so as not to ruin his chances at upward mobility, could no longer be kept silent. Our hero is now "woke," and he must ask himself, "Ignore the obvious, or let it in?"

Let's just say, Coates was my Morpheus, and his *not in it* was my red pill. And, for a while, life post-red pill sucked, because I could no longer do anything without the weight of race in it. At first, life outside the matrix can be kind of jarring. It was exhausting, I couldn't watch a movie, or go to the park with all the joggers and dog owners, or read the news, I couldn't get a haircut, or get a cup of coffee, go on a date, or order an avocado toast without seeing or hearing this *not in it-ness* in everything and everywhere.

Questions began to consume every inch of my life. Questions that challenged everything that whiteness, Blackness, and every otherness in between had taught me about my Brown body and my self-worth: Why is Brown *not in it*, and what's it going to take to not be trapped in the middle anymore? What are the physical ramifications of racism and not having a voice? What toll does desperation to be seen by a world that doesn't have a line for my shade take on my body?

I let the floodgates open, and I went from burden to celebration. Ignorance is bliss, they say, until you've *tasted* bliss, I say, and then the rest is just ignorance. This moment awoke me to what I couldn't see before, and I was forced to ask, "Ignore or let it in?" Personally speaking, ignoring would be far more painful than letting it in. Because then I would continue to be a part of the systemic problem.

In Buddhism, "understanding" is a powerful energy. Understanding might be the most powerful and necessary of all ingredients. It's understanding that turns irritation and anger into love. Understanding is that final ingredient in alchemy: the ability to turn nothing into something, to turn base metal into gold, to turn all my questions in my noisy mind into a quieter and more stable mind. Like Rilke says, "Love the questions themselves . . . and live yourself into an answer." When I lose faith, I return to alchemy. It gives me hope that radical transformation is possible. I'm not just talking personally, but politically, socially, systematically, with the climate, the possibility of a big alchemic shift gives me hope. I believe in the alchemy that arises from the power of understanding.

The alchemy that transforms *woe is me* into *yeah is us*.

Why does being in it matter so much to me? Because I am destined (maybe a little aggressively, but certainly pushed) to become the thing I see most, and it is much more difficult to become what I can't accurately see—a Brown president, a Brown hero, a Brown homeowner, a Brown person with a 401k and no student debt—a world where that is common and not extraordinary.

I watched a solo performance by playwright Brian Quijada called *Where Did We Sit on the Bus?* Brian tells the story of a question he once asked of a teacher when his class was learning about Rosa Parks during a Black History Month lesson. Looking around his public school room, he saw white kids and Black kids and wondered first to himself and then out loud to the teacher: "What about Brown Hispanic people, where were 'we' when all of this was going on? Where did we sit on the bus?" The room went silent. The teacher told him, "You weren't there." Not satisfied with the response he received, years later it became the inspiration for his play *Where Did We Sit on the Bus?*

Growing up in NYC, I have taken the bus hundreds of times. And let me tell you, whether it is NYC, LA, or another major city, the global majority are filling up them seats. According to a report by the American Public Transportation Association (APTA), "Communities of color make up a majority of riders," 60 percent to be exact.

Brian, I understand the feeling, I also know that it is impossible that we weren't there. On August 28, 1963, when MLK led the march on Washington, out of the 200,000 to 300,000 people who attended, thousands were Latinos—many of them Puerto Ricans from NYC. This is largely because MLK asked Gilberto Gerena Valentín, then president of the Puerto Rican Day Parade, to get the Latino population to turn out. For King, having a Latino presence was necessary. And the organizers gave Gerena fifteen minutes to address the crowd. He said to the masses, "There is discrimination not only against Blacks, but also against Puerto Ricans and Hispanics."

We were there when there were white water fountains and Black water fountains, white bathrooms, and Black bathrooms. We, Latinos, Native, Indigenous, Mixed, Middle Eastern, Asians, and other misunderstood and underrepresented minorities were there, facing discrimination, somewhere in the middle of Black and white, forced to pick a side.

In 2019, I was in a small mountain town in Switzerland on my way to a PhD program for expressive arts therapy that I have not yet finished. I was exhausted, I had already been travelling for thirteen hours and had about two hours left. My friend Mattia pulled the car over into a small falafel and fries shop on the side of a mountain. When we walked in, "Despacito," by Luis Fonsi, was blasting on the TV (up until recently it was the number one watched YouTube video of all time with just under eight billion views, until "Baby Shark" surpassed it in 2021). Everyone in the shop was singing it. Mattia, an Italian-born man, started singing it. When that song finished, another reggaeton song by J. Balvin popped on. Followed by an Ozuna track, and then Nicky Jam, and then Becky G, and the reggaeton party went on. I had to order my food by pointing at the picture I wanted because no one in the falafel shop spoke English, but I could at least rap with them in my mother's native tongue.

The German philosopher Georg Wilhelm Friedrich Hegel says, "In one way, we exist only to the extent that we are recognized by others." If that's true, then according to Coates's and Brian's teacher's rhetoric of "we were not there" and "still not in it," I do not exist. Hegel goes on to say, "A people is not a people unless its culture is recognized." But according to a falafel shop just outside of Saas-Fee, Switzerland, I definitely do exist because identity and Brownness and culture are beautiful and muddy like that.

As a kid who grew up in Queens, one of the most diverse places in this country, shit, maybe the world, I know that the palette of our nation will never be just one hue. I know that each and every one of us has a right to be recognized, accurately and truthfully, in the cultural landscape. I know that this lack of representation via images, media, politics, and culture limits and enlarges our notion of who counts in American society. I know that the work of decolonizing our minds from a white narrative that doesn't make space and include the shades and shades and shades and shades of Black, white, Brown, and every color in between is a daily one. A constant one, because the reach of colonization is far, wide, and deep.

I must now unlearn in order to understand. Understanding means letting go, listening, and allowing. Understanding is the practice of releasing. In America, globally, politically, socially, personally, romantically, locally, I believe it is good to practice letting go, walking into the unknown, and living with the ambiguity of what I don't yet know.

There is still a ton I don't know. I do know that on that evening in a library in Downtown LA, I was summoned to not just be a part of someone else's color line but to finally own and celebrate my own. Summoned by Brownness, my life was changed.

102-17 64th Road

"There is that in me—I do not know what it is—but I know
it is in me . . . I do not know it—it is without name—it
is a word unsaid, It is not in any dictionary, utterance,
symbol . . . It is not chaos or death—it is form, union,
plan—it is eternal life—it is Happiness."

—WALT WHITMAN,

LEAVES OF GRASS (1855)

1 02-17 64th Road, Queens, was the place to be. That
building was more than a childhood home, its inhab-
itants more than neighbors. It was a school. It was a
lifeline. It was my people. It was my family. Family that went
way beyond my mother, my father, and my sister. The building was a kingdom, and I was the prince because my father
was the super king. Or the superintendent, or whatever you
like to call it, and between his two pagers (pre-cellphone) and
his three hundred keys on the biggest key ring you have ever
seen, he knew everything, everybody, and everything about
everybody.

We can't move further until I lay down the foundation of my
home. I'd be remiss if I did not give props to the other 164 brothers and sisters and mothers and fathers I had in that building.

Mrs. Butt—yes, that was her actual name—was a fabulous elder who got her college degree at eighty-four. She lived on the first floor, in the first apartment right when you walked into the building, and she would sing late at night, crooning old-school songs as loud as she could because she refused to wear her hearing aids. You could basically hear her TV playing reruns of *The Golden Girls* from outside the building. Anytime she saw me, she would shout, "Chris, come here!" She would pull out a bunch of pennies and a tennis ball. I had so many tennis balls I could have sponsored the US Open. Every time I would yell back to thank her, just to make sure she heard me, she'd get mad and ask, "Why are you yelling!?"

Apartment 1J was where all the magic happened, where I came home right after the hospital, New York-Presbyterian— same hospital my pops was born in. It was a tiny one-bedroom that all four of us shared. My sister and I shared the bedroom and my parents had the living room. They set up this sweet Murphy bed (you know the kind that fold up flush into the wall when not being used) and partitioned the living room in two halves using a sliding curtain and a partial wall that my pops built. My pops's real pride and joy was the hundred-gallon fish tank that he installed into that partial wall, which separated the living room/living room and my parents' bedroom/living room. 1J is where my mom spent a lot of time laid up on her stomach because she had fallen off a horse while visiting her brother in Miami. It herniated some discs in her back, which required multiple spinal surgeries. This is why I used to walk around the city not stepping on cracks. Because you know the phrase, "Step on a crack, you break your mama's back?" Yeah, well I believed that shit.

When I was eight, my pops was still the super, but we'd been there long enough that when a two-bedroom finally became available, we got an upgrade. Apartment 4A was where my parents finally had their own bedroom with a door and everything. Again, there were four of us—now my parents got a room (much deserved), my sister got a room (less deserved), and I got a partitioned part of the living room (plain unfair). I did get to decide how I wanted to build the wall between me and the living room. I chose glass blocks, real 80s drug dealer-like. It was sweet.

Right above our apartment was my sister's best friend. We were pretty tight with their family, they kept nothing a secret, not sure they could if they wanted to. We knew everything—the very loud fights, the time one of the girls ran away to our house, the time the oldest daughter got a Dominican guy to convert to Judaism and get an adult circumcision. Yes, he cut off his foreskin for her—now, that is love.

Across the other side of the building was 6J, that's where Danny lived, my best friend in the whole world. A brother more than a friend. I spent close to as many nights at his house as I did in my own place, he did the same at mine. He loved my place because we had salami and for a kid growing up in Queens who had never had salami, it was a very big deal.

When I was thirteen, I saved up a bunch of money, maybe forty dollars (that was a lot back then), so that I could buy Danny a remote for his PlayStation. He never got to open it. Three days before Christmas, Danny was hit by a car while crossing the street on his way to an orthodontist appointment. He wasn't dead right away, more like brain dead. When I got to the hospital waiting room, my pain poured out as rage. I was furious, I started punching walls and screaming. My father and mother who were also in pain, did their best to restrain me, telling me, "We understand. We're mad, too. It sucks. But this isn't the way."

That night I had multiple opportunities to walk into the actual ICU room and see his face. As I'd imagined it, a battered and bruised face, a misshapen skull, and eyes that might or might not have recognized me beyond the brain damage. I tried to walk in, I made it about three steps into the room before I turned around and ran. I hit a wall of fear I couldn't move past. Was I protecting myself from an image I couldn't handle? Or haunting myself with an image I still can't unsee?

I couldn't go to school. I couldn't do much of anything. I didn't cry but I did get angry. I punched a lot of walls, tried to start a lot of fights. Looking at my knuckles right now I know that they are still bruised and scarred from that time.

After his funeral, I didn't go to another funeral for fifteen years.

For a year after we lost him, I couldn't sleep. I was haunted by these epic nightmares of death. I would wake up crying and screaming, and my mother would rush to my room to sit and pray with me, she prayed more over me and for me than with me.

I am still wildly afraid of death. There are nights where I am afraid to the point of a full-on panic attack—a racing heart and me staring up at the ceiling knowing that one day all this will end . . . and then what?

During that time there was a therapist who lived in the building. My parents wanted me to see her. Even though now my father says, "Oh her, she's the one who needed therapy," back then, it's what we had. I said I'd go, but I just went for long walks, instead. When they made me go, and walked me to her door, I kept quiet and said nothing.

Throughout that time, people from this building would often visit me, check in on me. They would bring me treats, ask me how I was doing, see if I wanted to go for a walk. I'd appreciated the gesture, but they couldn't do anything to bring him back.

The year that Danny died was the first time I contemplated suicide and my own mortality. I was thirteen years old, crying and sitting on the floor of the kitchen with a pair of dull scissors in my hand. I wasn't exactly sure how I could use them, or how I would, but I knew I could. I knew that death was this close, death was sitting in my left hand.

Holding those scissors was my first taste of realizing this isn't a life you have to live but rather a life you choose to live. Knowing that you get to pull the plug at any instant became a powerful truth.

A year later, I started my freshman year at a specialized high school for the performing arts. Talent Unlimited.

Yeah, I know, we used to make fun of the school name too. We would call it T.U. because Talent Unlimited felt like the name you give a place to make people feel like they were special or talented, when, actually, they weren't. Everyone knows that the preeminent performing arts high school in New York is LaGuardia . . . Al Pacino went there, Billy Dee Williams, Jennifer Aniston. I applied for that school, too.

I didn't get into LaGuardia, which is really their loss. LaGuardia might have had Pacino and Rachel from *Friends*, but T.U. was where Laurence Fishburne (Morpheus for Christ's sake), Mos Def, and *moi*—Christopher Rivas—went. Despite its funny name, T.U. was still a performing arts school, and the beginning of my formal training. But before that training could really get underway, on my fourth day as a freshman, September 11, 2001, the World Trade Center was struck by two planes.

Inside the school we had no real idea what was happening downtown. The teachers were freaking out. My math teacher's mother and wife were both in one of the towers. Everyone could feel the panic. Teachers kept walking in and out of the classroom. The phones were all just getting busy signals. Every parent in New York City was trying to call someone. The school couldn't let us leave; they couldn't just send us outside into the crumbling world until they had more answers.

It was terrifying. So, me and the other kids leaned on each other. It was only day four, but we got to really know each other.

I was just wandering the hallways with my homie Tyler when I heard my name. It was Danny's father. He hadn't connected with my parents, the phone lines were all down, he just decided to walk forty or so blocks to see if I was still in school because that's what family does.

I'll be honest, him and I had done our fair share of avoiding each other after Danny died. Seeing one another reminded each of us of Danny and that was painful. I was shocked to see him.

"How you doing?" he asked.

"Confused . . . Happy you're here."

"Me too. Both confused and happy I'm here with you. What do you say we go home?"

We first stopped into a diner on Second Avenue and he bought me a burger. With the confusion of everything and the giant black cloud of smoke covering the island, that burger tasted like nothing at all. And then we made the long trek across the 59th Street Bridge all the way back to our building in Queens.

When we made it across the bridge, there were a ton of people with water and paper towels, it was hot out, everyone was out, people were giving out hugs and support however they could. When I got back to the building everyone who wasn't watching the news was on the front stoop checking on people, praying. It felt like everybody knew somebody who was in those buildings. My parents were terrified. Everyone was so relieved to see me walk through the door. We didn't really talk because there was still so much confusion and uncertainty about what was happening. We just hugged and waited to learn more.

That was pretty much the last time I saw Danny's parents. They tried to move on from the loss of their son, but the building held too many memories. They moved from Queens to Portland, to Morocco, and on, and on.

Before they left the building, we had a small but generous goodbye. Danny's parents gave me a cassette tape Danny had recorded for me. He was experimenting with hypnosis. About a year later, when I finally listened to it, I realized I had forgotten his voice. Think about that, the length of time it takes to forget a voice, their timbre, love, and depth. To this day, I keep a few chosen voicemails around, just in case I lose them, and there is a voice I don't want to forget.

There was no school for a week, and then the trains opened up again and I was back at T.U., back on my big dream and acting grind, and, once again, very aware that in an instant, everything could change. This reminder that it can all go just like that, is likely one of the reasons I decided to pursue acting with my whole everything, even when it felt impossible, because if it could crumble in an instant, I might as well love it while it's happening.

A couple floors below Danny's family was my French, bisexual, pastry chef godfather. He had this outstanding passion for life and the thickest French accent you have ever heard. I was amazed that I could even understand him; it is a special skill acquired over time. I looked up to him and his commitment to being a pastry chef, his dedication was something I could relate to as an artist. In this incarnation, he was dating a man, but before that he was married twice to women. "You love who you love, just make sure to love," he'd tell me. Being around this freedom of love, freedom of choice, at such a young age was really special. It was never named or defined or categorized, it just was, and we all loved what was. My godfather was the best person to have in the family, not just because he made these delicious desserts, but also because he's one of the most inspiring people I know. I watched him go from restaurant chef to having a pastry empire. I even worked my first job ever there, washing dishes and serving gelato.

Across from my godfather was his boyfriend, a music executive who worked for Arista Records. Every Tuesday he would bring me and my pops a fat stack of new music to listen to. Before Spotify, Tuesdays were when new records came out. My pops and I would spend hours listening to these albums, not really speaking, not bouncing around from track to track, just one CD at a time, cross-legged, and eating Oreos with milk (I wasn't lactose intolerant yet). Music of all kinds, like Kriss Kross, who I loved so much that I used to wear my clothes backward just like them, until one family party when I almost peed my pants because I almost didn't get them off in time.

A Tribe Called Quest, Nas (when I wrote this, my computer didn't think Nas was a word), Mobb Deep, Biggie, Jay Z, Mos &

Talib, Boyz II Men, 112, Next, Jodeci, B2K, Immature—a group of basically thirteen-year-olds singing about love. Why we as a society love little boys singing about love is beyond my comprehension; but we do, and I sure did.

Every Tuesday, I would spend hours listening and reading those amazing album pamphlets back to front, front to back. Studying the lyrics and the nuances of keeping it cool and letting it all go.

Our door was always open. This isn't an exaggeration, my folks loved hosting and being social. All the time people would just come over and hang, and this is when I would put my music knowledge and need to be a showman to the test, I would perform these lip sync renditions of totally inappropriate songs for a twelve-year-old to be singing to guests, like Az Yet's, "Last Night" with lyrics that intimately describe a man making love to a woman, including what it feels like to be inside said woman. Yes, I sang that with a large wooden cooking spoon to a lot of my parents' friends. People loved it. I got standing ovations. My best showstopping performance was of Mary J. Blige's "Not Gon' Cry," from the *Waiting to Exhale* soundtrack. This would explain why in my adult years I have won three lip-syncing competitions. I can't sing for shit, but I can lip sync with the best of 'em.

It wasn't just R&B, it was bachata, salsa, disco, soul, house, I loved it all. The queen for me was and still is Sade! When I first heard her, it was this soft, kind of trance-like, ucky-gooky, crazy romantic, bathtub music—and I hated it. I was ready to switch CDs not even halfway through, but my pops shut that down real quick. So, I sat back and huffed and puffed, rolled my eyes, and sucked my teeth as Sade and her velvet voice began to take over my body. I swear, I felt it wash over me, turn me, move me, every track better than the last; but I refused to show my pops that I liked what we were listening to, so I kept my stank face on the whole time—like I'm smelling shit in the air, but on the inside, it's actually roses, big fat, real-smelling roses filled with sexy music.

Later that night, when everyone was asleep, I walked into the living room, grabbed the CD, popped it into my computer, ripped it onto my iTunes, and listened to *Lovers Rock* every day for weeks, I still know every song by heart.

Living right above my godfather's boyfriend, the music-gifting god, was my father's sister, her two cats, my niece, and my grandmother.

In 2003, when I was sixteen, I was walking home from a friend's house when I noticed an odd commotion in the streets. I walked into the corner 7-Eleven and noticed there was no power.

I asked the guy behind the counter, "How long's this been going on for?"

"A couple hours and it's the whole city," he informed me.

This was the epic blackout of 2003.

Obviously, before I ran home, I asked him, "My man, you down to part with some free ice cream and or a slushie? It's hot as hell and it's all gonna melt anyway."

He looked at me like I was crazy . . . but I held my stare and didn't back down . . . "Only one," he said.

I chose ice cream.

When I got back home my whole building was just chillin' on the front stoop.

That night, in the hot, muggy summer darkness of NYC, a couple folks pulled their cars out onto the street, one here, one there, and they each had their headlights facing the stoop. Then everyone had their radios tuned into the same radio station—probably Hot 97 or WBLS, with real surround sound bumping. Everyone brought down the food that was going to go bad in the fridge, they brought out their little charcoal grills and started grilling.

We danced salsa, we played dominoes, we talked about Mrs. Butt, wondering if she would have joined had she been alive. All the kids brought down tennis balls in her honor. We played spades, we played 500 rummy. We danced some more and had a good old family block party.

That building was my family. The home where I watched my father throw a man through the front glass window because he was hurting one of the women in the building. He was defending his family. My family, our family, not by blood, but by home, by spirit. And the rest of the hundred and sixty families in the building backed him up immediately because that's what you do for a family. You pray together when the man downstairs dies unexpectedly, or when the family in 2G needs you to make sure that they don't open the door for their heroin addict son. You fight across the hallway when you want quiet, you fight very loudly and then you gossip about it the next day with everybody. But also, you connect tables across the hallway, stacking tables like a snake that make it out the front door, connecting into someone else's apartment so that sixty people can share a Thanksgiving dinner, one that starts in one apartment for the first course, moves to a couple other apartments for the second, and then another for dessert (yes, at my godfather's). In this building my entire extended family had thin walls, big ass mouths, and even bigger hearts. Why else do you think I went to forty different Hanukkah parties, forty Christmas parties, and a couple of Kwanzaas (that's just in one year), because everyone in the family was always celebrating something.

There was always a birthday party and there was always a barbecue. We shoved thirty people into our tiny apartment for an "intimate dinner." Everyone was our babysitter. My parents were so comfortable with this building family that they left the country for a month and trusted that all these people would just show up and watch my sister and me. They did. This included them driving us to the hospital when my sister needed to get stitches in her hand because she accidently put her hand through the bathroom window, and another hospital trip for a terrible case of food poisoning my sister got from an old pork chop. Both times, the family was there.

Then, one day, it was time to go. I was eighteen and my folks were done. My pops said, "I will never shovel snow again." He and my mom did what many Latino snowbirds do, and they flew south to Miami, the land of the Cuban sandwich and a cheap *cafecito*.

I had just finished high school and, honestly, I was pretty lost. I had no idea about what was next for me. So, I went with them and became a personal trainer in South Beach (but that's another story for another time).

That melting pot of a building in Queens was the foundation for all that was to come next. It laid the roots for so much that I would come to fight for in this life. It showed me the importance of community and diversity. How very different people, from very different backgrounds can love each other, and take care of one another. And that difference is in essence, Brownness. Brownness honors unique identities rooted in race and ethnicity

rather than whiteness that embraces assimilation and marginal-
izes any deviance from a sinisterly crafted default ideal. That
building and my time there was a tiny universe on what it means
to be human. We can be shitty and kill each other and do all
sorts of horrible things but we can also show up and care for one
another—yes, we *can* love thy neighbor.

"Family," according to Webster's, is a group consisting of parents and children living together in a household, descendants of
a common ancestor. In this case, our family's common ancestor
was the 164-unit large melting pot building located at 102-17
64th Rd. Queens, New York, 11375. And that family and I, we
rolled deep. I loved them. I will always love them.

Mejorando La Raza—
What's in My Blood?

"A silent anonymous influence, a bit like the way our
ancestors blood moves incessantly within us and
combines with our own to form the unique, unrepeatable
being that we are at every turn in our life."

—RAINER MARIA RILKE,
LETTERS TO A YOUNG POET (1929)

I had recently been teaching a storytelling workshop, and after class, this young, fit, attractive white woman in yoga pants and a vintage T-shirt came up to me to thank me. She told me that the workshop had really resonated with her, explaining how one of the free writes we did confirmed that she was really ready to make a change and move into life transformation, health, and wellness coaching (yes, I live in Los Angeles). She said she was finally ready to help people manifest their dreams, and she knew this made sense because she had just gotten back her 23andMe results and said, and I quote, "I have some South Asian in me, and that makes total sense because I connect with that part of the world in my soul."

I froze. I froze in part disbelief, part shock, because this is not the first time this has happened to me. I don't ask for it. I don't invite it. It just happens. White people love telling me that they aren't as white as I might think they are. They *love* it. Like a badge of honor that says: "Beneath this skin is so much more. I'm like a tenth Middle Eastern." Or "There's actually a little bit of Africa in there [the whole continent?]." Or "It was wild, I could have sworn I was some white mutt, but there is like a sprinkle of 14 percent sub-Saharan African in there, no for real, it's true. Even some [insert other darker skinned nation and place of origin here]."

It feels like some sort of badge of honor, a get out of jail free card, a way to say, "I knew I wasn't one of those racists participating in all the racist stuff that happens all the time, everywhere. I knew I was different."

And if it's not directly to me, then I'll hear it in some sort of park, coffeeshop, natural wine bar—basically there isn't a space in Los Angeles where I haven't heard one white person say to another: "I just did my ancestry. Have you done yours? What's in your blood?"

I have not done a 23andMe as I don't feel one hundred percent comfortable with giving my DNA to a private company (as if they don't already have it). That said, I love that question, "What's in my blood?"

What's in my blood?

It wasn't something I'd really thought of before. My dad is Dominican, my mom is Colombian, I was born and raised in Queens, I ate food from both cultures, danced their respective dances, and listened to their respective music. All of this worked for me. Until it didn't.

The Dominican Republic was the first seat of Spanish colonial rule in the New World. The DR was actually the first place in the Americas that Christopher Columbus landed, and, obviously, he and other colonizers *decimated* the Indigenous population. In fact, the Dominican Republic was the first place in the new world where Africans were imported to become slaves.

Yes, slavery is in my blood. Ninety percent of Dominicans descend from West African slaves. Yet, few Dominicans self-identify as Black; the majority identify as "mestizo" or "Indio," preferring to acknowledge only their European and Indigenous heritage. Maybe this is why there is a porcelain white statue of Columbus in the center of the capital, Santo Domingo. Because most Dominicans believe with all their hearts that they are white and Spanish.

On the island of Hispaniola, a shared island between the Dominican Republic and Haiti, Spain implemented a caste system that placed folks who were of European or mixed European descent higher on the social ladder and allowed them more opportunities to advance. Though this system no longer exists, there are still heavy traces of it today. In many countries all over the world, color is linked to status, education, income, and class. Darker skin signifies inferiority and people who may work in agriculture, construction, or anything that exposes them to outdoor elements like the sun. Lighter skin tones represent superiority and individuals who work in offices and in what would be considered "good jobs," coming from "good families."

Other members of my family always had fairer skin, thinner hair, and smaller lips and noses. Somehow I came out with the biggest lips, the biggest nose, and the curliest and thickest hair. As a kid, my family was always joking about me being adopted. I knew it was a joke, but sometimes jokes aren't actually that funny. Sometimes jokes just make you feel your difference even more. There were days where I really did think I was adopted.

As a child, my thick, Afro-Latino, textured hair was often referred to as *pelo malo*, the "bad hair" in the family. Referring to my hair as "bad" was not meant to be mean, it was seen as a fact. Hair that isn't straight and thin is just more of the African we are trying to hide. Because like skin color, hair is also social currency. This is why growing up, the women around me were obsessed with straight, silky hair. It's why I spent hours in salons with the very unique smell of hot, heat infused, just on the edge of burning hair. Heat in order to tame it because hair can easily give you away. My Dominican homegirl, an actress who is also from New York, who recently decided to let her hair go natural, over a glass of happy hour wine said to me, "I haven't put heat in my hair in three months, and my mind feels cooler."

There are dark-skinned Dominicans, *moreno*, which literally means "dark-skinned." And many Dominicans choose to call themselves *moreno* and not Black because identifying as Black is still widely frowned upon in that community. It's an insult, worse than kicking your mother. In the DR, there is no worse insult than to be called Black. The darker-skinned members of my family were often ridiculed with demeaning words like *mona*, meaning monkey. I once watched my pops's friend call my grandmother Black, not out of spite, but out of solidarity. His exact words as he went in for a hug were, "Come here, my Black sister"—and it was like he spat in her face—a rage unlike any I'd ever seen.

Deeper—what's in my blood?

A heavy dose of colorism and *mejorando la raza*—an all-too common phrase used in many Latin American countries, it means "improving" or "bettering the race." It suggests that it would be wise to marry or have children with a whiter person.

Not white-white, I mean if you are lucky, sure, but the focus is on becoming closer to whiteness, lightening the lineage by being with someone with lighter skin and eyes than you. This way your kids will have more of an opportunity for upward mobility. It emphasizes the fact that skin color is a social currency, light skin is valuable, and darkness is not.

As a child, it was instilled in me that lighter was always better than being darker. I saw this at family parties, I saw this in school, I saw this with my grandmother, and the many grandmothers, mothers, grandfathers, and fathers around me who would all warn us: "Don't date someone darker than you. Date someone *que se ve fino*. Date someone with that fair skin."

I could see and feel the benefits of being lighter, the compliments, the praise, the hope in their eyes that this person closer to whiteness might be a pathway to a "better" life. I saw it everywhere, even if I couldn't verbalize it.

This *mejorando la raza*, this obsession with intergenerational whitening, is deep in my blood. It comes from generations before me and will likely exist generations after me, and it crosses many borders. In the Dominican Republic, this white savior mentality has been trying, and is still trying, to eliminate black skin color and any vestige of African ancestry and culture altogether.

Because in my blood is the overnight genocide and racist massacre of 20,000–30,000 Haitians—people from the same land, the same island, Hispaniola, because Haitians are the Black ones on the island. In my blood is a culture that hates the other side of the island. So much so that Dominicans celebrate their independence from Haiti, not from their colonizer Spain (remember the Columbus statue in the capital). Reminds me of the Baldwin quote, "It becomes clear—for some—that the more closely one resembles the invader, the more comfortable one's life may become."

(And who doesn't want comfort?)

The Parsley Massacre of 1937 was executed by Rafael Trujillo (one of the bloodiest dictators in Latin American history). Trujillo ordered that all Haitian men, women, and children be rounded up, beaten, and hacked to death. Even dark-skinned Dominicans were murdered in "el corte," the cutting—a movement of extermination.

According to Trujillo, Haitians crossing the border were a problem, Haitians taking jobs on Dominican farms were a problem. Here's an excerpt from a speech Trujillo gave in 1937—marking the beginning of the massacre:

I have seen, investigated, and inquired about the needs of the population. To the Dominicans who were complaining of the depredations by Haitians living among them, thefts of cattle, provisions, fruits, etc., and were thus prevented from enjoying in peace the products of their labor, I have responded, "I will fix this." And we have already begun to remedy the situation. Three hundred Haitians are now dead in Bánica. This remedy will continue.

Remedy. He called it a "remedy."

According to the Jungian idea of the shadow, there are aspects of ourselves we find unacceptable, and we project these things onto external enemies. We are afraid to become the thing we are. Carl Jung says:

Unfortunately there can be no doubt that man is, on the whole, less good than he imagines himself or wants to be. Everyone carries a shadow, and the less it is embodied in the individual's conscious life, the blacker and denser it is.

Unsurprisingly, Trujillo himself had Haitian ancestry. A Haitian grandmother. Spent time there as a child. This Dominican dictator with Haitian family and Haitian blood powdered his skin and whitened his face with baby powder multiple times a day because he was so obsessed with believing the lie that he was white. He was so afraid that he wasn't white enough and so afraid of being found out that he banned people from ever leaving the island. He attempted daily to get rid of any semblance of Blackness left in him and on the island, by banning bachata and any music that was related to the DR's Black history.

In her book *Meeting the Shadow*, Connie Zweig, renowned expert in human psychology, writes:

The shadow goes by many familiar names: the disowned self, the lower self, the dark twin or brother in bible and myth, the double, repressed self, alter ego, id. When we come face-to-face with our darker side, we use metaphors to describe these shadow encounters: meeting our demons, wrestling with the devil, descent to the underworld, dark night of the soul, midlife crisis.

Seems unfair to always have to cast our shadow into a dark light. What comes from Brown people proudly claiming their shadow? Not casting the shadow into darkness but embracing that it is a companion with whom to walk side by side. That shadow is never going anywhere, no matter how much baby powder you use.

The craziest part is something my father recently told me. Apparently, somewhere in my bloodline is my great grandfather, Juan Alba, a man I'd never heard about until my thirty-fourth year, who was one of the founders of a small town in the DR called La Caleta. I was shocked that I hadn't been told this sooner. I mean, creating a town is a big deal. I asked my pops, "What else don't I know?" Turns out, Juan Alba was a cousin-in-law to Rafael Trujillo—yeah, that Trujillo. The guy known as one of the bloodiest dictators in history. Trujillo was married to María de los Ángeles Martínez Alba. That was my great grandfather's cousin.

On the one hand, I'm not *that* surprised about being related to Trujillo. The DR is a tiny island. It's kind of a joke that everyone on the island are cousins. But, on the other hand, it does feel crazy that I'm connected to Trujillo. Maybe not by blood-blood, but still. It is an unpleasant part of my family tree. And that's just one half of me I have to reconcile.

On the other side of me is the blood that pours down from a vibrant melodic and lively place known as Colombia. A place full of magnificent color and music. It's beautiful, and it's one of the most biodiverse countries in the world. The streets are alive, the buildings have stunning blues, sharp oranges, and magnificent reds.

At thirty years old, I flew myself to Bogotá, Columbia, for the first time. A solo trip. I wanted to return to my mother's birthland. I wanted to be alone with the roots that are in my blood. As soon I landed there, this peace washed over me. All of a sudden, I was no longer pretending, I was resting—resting in my blood, resting in my skin. I wasn't Brown, I wasn't special or exotic, I was just me.

I walked into the first museum I could find, looked at the paintings, looked at the sculptures, looked at the patrons, and I thought: "I have survived. My face has survived." I thought, and still think: "Back home, we are erasing Brown people, our people. Slowly. Systematically. Effectively. We are erasing people."

As I moved throughout Colombia, I realized erasure took place there as well, that they suffered the same fate as my Dominican blood. Another Spanish conquest that brought over a million Africans to become slaves in Colombia—where, over time, Black and darker skinned bodies were pushed to the periphery, to remote and depressed areas; where, to this day, they are forgotten by the government; where basic needs are unmet, public services are lacking, and education is of low quality. In my blood is the common Colombian assumption that dark-skinned people are poor, while fair-skinned people are thriving.

I see irony in the fact that such colorful places can have such hatred of color.

Cali, the third most populated city in the country (after Bogotá and Medellín) has the largest Black population. Cali is 70 percent Black. In fact, Cali is referred to as "Chocolate City," a moniker also given to Washington, DC. How similar are we?

In my blood are dark complected Latinos that hate their even darker complected Latino neighbors. There are dark complected Latinos that hate their *lighter* complected Latino neighbors. And there are white Latinos that look at anyone with skin darker than theirs like they're not worthy, like they're making all the other ones look bad, like they are making it harder for everyone else. It's an endless cycle that reminds me that we have been associating improvement and upward mobility with whiteness for a very long time.

In my blood are the 136 terms for different skin colors in Brazil. That's 136 different colors and racial categories. Including *alverente*—which roughly translates to "shadow in the water." That's a skin color and the name of my next band. Or *acastanhada*—somewhat chestnut-colored; *alva*—snowy white; *alva escura*—dark snowy white; *alvarinto*—kind of blonde; *alva rosada*—pinkish white; *amorenada*—somewhat dark-skinned; *avermelhada*—reddish; *azul*—blue; *bem morena*—very dark-skinned; *bem branca*—very white; *branca-avermelhada*—white going for red; *branca-melada*—honey-colored white; *branca-morena*—white but dark-skinned; *bronzeada*—sun-tanned; *bugrezinha-escura*—dark-skinned Indian; *cor-de-canela*—cinnamon-colored; *cor-de-cuia*—gourd-colored (and we're only in the Cs, y'all).

Ironically, Brazil, now has a new law that gives more government jobs to Black Brazilians. The catch, though, is that anyone who wants one of these jobs has to prove to a panel of judges that he or she qualifies. That he or she is Black enough. They have committees where they're literally measuring people's nose width, testing, and measuring skull shape and nose width to see who's Black and who's white.

Now Brown Brazilians aren't looking toward whiteness but fighting to prove their Blackness, a thing once ignored.

In my blood are the sixty different shades used to describe Black in Cuba. Sixty. In my blood are the thirty names for color in Central America—*castizo, mestizo, coyote,* and perhaps the most fucked-up term, *para-tras. Para-tras* is basically when you say to a person: "Yo, you were almost white, but then you took a step back. *Para-tras.*"

I don't look toward anything in my blood, my ancestral mathematics, the twelve previous generations of more than four thousand ancestors, and all their struggles, love, battles, and hopes for the future for reassurance of who I am. I don't seek comfort; I seek honest revelation.

I don't look to the Dominican annihilation and genocide of Haitians for years and years, or the forced conversions of the Spanish, the raping and pillaging, or the Brown bodies' obsession with fitting in with the standards of their European colonizer to say look how far we've come but rather to see why we are so distorted, inherently racist, and defined before we even open our eyes and take our first breaths.

In a Eurocentric, colonized, white body–run culture, melanin is an illness for which there is no cure. If people of color want freedom and power (which we *all* do), we must despise the thing we are. And so, me and little Brown boys and girls take in the information sold to us. We try to tuck and hide our different features and put all sorts of products in our hair and on our skin because we have been force-fed what gaze really matters.

To some extent, I need the white gaze to admire me, because I want to be successful to the mainstream eye, and the mainstream eye is still the white eye. I am an artist, I went to theater school, I write, I have a ton of student loan debt, I make a living acting in the machine known as Hollywood—an industry that commodifies me but isn't for me. An industry where if I am using my hands too much on camera, the director shouts out in all seriousness, "Not so much of the ethnic hands!"

"White hands, Chris, white hands," I whisper to myself while smiling.

The essence of what I do is put myself in spaces where I must be chosen, where I must be selected as worthy enough to portray this thing. Beyond the ability to act, a large portion has to do with whether I am physically aesthetically appealing and pleasing enough to a certain gaze. When you make a living off your desirability, is the power of your body ever just yours? My body has been turned into an object of desire by whiteness, and as long as the main decision-makers and check signers in Hollywood are white bodies, then I must be desirable to and for them. In my opinion, this is the other side of the same coin of being seen as worthless. Because if I am not desirable in some way, then I am worthless. And I fear that if I change too radically from what they have already deemed acceptable, then I might lose whatever status I have already worked so hard to achieve.

I just might not survive.

Sammy Sosa, the homerun slugging former major league baseball player from the Dominican Republic who whitened his skin, is not an enigma. He is a public-facing believer of the lie, of the story about which gaze matters, and he is doing his best to wear the costume that he has been told he should wear. In an interview with *Primer Impacto* on the Univision network that you can easily find on YouTube, Sammy says nonchalantly to the reporter when asked about his skin being lighter, "It's a bleaching cream that I apply before going to bed, and it whitens my skin some," as if it's no big deal. My feeling on Sammy's situation is similar to learning that Trujillo powdered his skin: sadness for Sosa, sadness for Trujillo. Because they didn't *invent* this notion, and they didn't decide to hate themselves . . . It's in the blood. Whether it's Sammy Sosa, Trujillo, Michael Jackson, or the many other believers of the lie, they inherited this pain, and they couldn't unlearn it. They are a warning about how far some will go to prove that they are good enough to be seen.

Like spending a manageable thirty-five dollars on the famous "Nose Secret" tool, often advertised as "plastic surgery, without the surgery." It is a plastic tubing that you manually insert and force into your nose to create a narrower, thinner, and more pointed shape. At only thirty-five dollars, it's a steal!

We consider those who commit self-harm to themselves a danger to themselves and to society. We criminalize that act. But what about self-hate?

Who is there to protect us from that? Who is there to tell us that our skin must be guarded against bleach and that our darker pigment means that we are made for the sun, not to hide from it? How many of us can actually say, "I have a beautiful body, in its original form"?

I ask these questions about my own blood, I do the research, I visit the places, I challenge my family, and/or I spit in a tube (yes, I succumb to the genealogical curiosity), and, yes, unarmed Black people are still shot in the back at point blank seven times in front of their children. Someone not being *fully* white doesn't solve anything. Brown, white, Black, a DNA breakdown doesn't absolve me from stepping up and taking action. And it doesn't absolve you. No percentage of Indigenous blood means that I am released from using my voice right here and now, and my pie chart doesn't give me a free pass into understanding someone's plight.

What's in my blood is a painful experience of trying to survive in a world not made for me. Woven into my DNA is an ancient wound that I share with much of humanity. Something that Ancestry.com and 23andMe doesn't make it any easier for me to understand.

I also know there is medicine and guidance in all this. I know there is strength in my blood, perseverance, craftiness, and the ability to be more loving and more kind in the face of hate. What's in my blood is not just ancestral hurt trauma, it's not only the dark side of epigenetics. It's also the courage to disconnect and heal from the white gaze. Toni Morrison said, "I have spent my entire writing life trying to make sure that the white gaze was not the dominant one in any of my books."

Did I respond to the woman who said, "I have some South Asian in me . . . I connect with that part of the world in my soul"?

I did.

"I gotta stop you," I said. "Because blood is tricky. A ton of it was taken and spilled violently so we could be here right now. I am not telling you to not learn about yourself and where you come from, but it's never so simple as Brown, Black, white, a quarter Asian, a fifth Native American, and look where my ancestors are from. So, maybe you can also share with me how the state of the world *boils your blood*, and what you're going to do about it."

Because regardless of my blood, where I am from, and where I am going, I still have work to do. Racism is a public health issue, a public issue, an "all of ours" issue. We all matter or none of us do, and every time another person of culture is murdered simply for just being, our humanity, the very definition of what it means to be human, takes the hit.

Words Are Spells
in Your Mouth

"Do not be satisfied with the stories that come before
you. Unfold your own myth."

— RUMI

O n my twenty-sixth birthday I was performing in a play in
Los Angeles and my mom had just been admitted to the
ICU. Her pancreas had suddenly decided to take some
time off and rest a little. The thing about the pancreas is we don't
really know why it does or doesn't want to work. That's it.
There's no replacement pancreas in the wings, no transplants, no
drugs. There's just assistance, a lot of prayer, and a patient's hope.

I had no idea this happened because my parents decided not
to tell me at first. The play was about Frida Kahlo (my mother's
favorite artist) and her love affair with Leon Trotsky. I played a
neighbor who knew the juicy details, and it was a lot of fun.
When my pops finally told me what was going on back home, I
was ready to book a flight that minute, but then my mom hopped
on the phone and said in the softest voice I've ever heard from
her, "I want you to finish the run, I need you to finish the show."

"No, definitely not, I'm coming home," I said.

"If you leave early, that means we're running out of time, that means we're all giving up hope, and I am not giving up hope." Then she hit me with: "Don't worry, I'll still be here for all your shows. Finish this show. I'm not going nowhere."

I finished the show, my mom ended up spending twenty-six days in the ICU, she recovered, and now she's doing great.

In its simplest form, the stage is where someone who looks like me can see and be their whole selves. It is a place where we can become everything and anything. Free from the nagging feeling and the baggage of "I am not enough." On that stage I've been a romantic, a composer, a soldier, a wolf, a child, a Trojan warrior, a vaudevillian star, a crippled king, a French poet. On that stage, it wasn't just stereotypes, traumas, and woe-is-me up there but also the joys, complexities, and fullness of our beings.

I am trying to remember this feeling of enough, this freedom to be myself, while in a rehearsal room in Dallas as I repeat for the twelfth time a line from the play I wrote, "Proudly, in my own Brown Skin."

"One more time please," says Daniel Banks, my director and friend.

"Proudly, in my own Brown Skin," I repeat.

"I'm sorry," he says, "I just can't hear it. Why can't I hear it? You are saying it, but I can't hear it."

We were in the middle of rehearsing (which I like to think of as "re-hear-ing") a one-man show I wrote and still perform around the country titled *The Real James Bond . . . Was Dominican!*

I, too, am Dominican. You know this if you've made it this far. I'm proud of this. At least, I thought I was proud of this. I thought I had done the work to own my own words, "Proudly, in my own Brown Skin."

"Nope, I can't hear it, why can't I hear it?" Daniel asks. "Funny, you've been saying it, but I'm not hearing it. Why can't I hear it?"

I know it's a rhetorical question, obviously he hasn't lost his hearing all of a sudden. He can hear just fine.

What he meant to say was, he couldn't feel it. Even more, what he meant to say was, he didn't believe it. And if he didn't believe it, there is a good chance, neither did I.

That's the thing about theater—it's hard to lie to someone, the audience can feel the lie immediately. They can smell the pretend.

Daniel asks me, "Are you actually proud?"

"Proud?"

"Yes, proud. Proud of your Brown skin? Are you actually proud of your Brown skin? You say it, but are you *actually* Proud, like with a capital 'P' *Proud*? I think that's why I don't hear it; you sound remorseful when you say it. Right now, I hear sorrow. But it's 'Proudly,' you wrote 'Proudly.'"

I did write "Proudly." He's right.

That's his joke whenever I flub one of my own lines that I wrote. He says, "Yo, I just spoke with the writer, he told me to tell you to stop fucking up the words."

And I wrote "Proudly." Still, in that moment, once again I am reminded, that sometimes we write checks about self-worth that our bodies are still trying to cash. In that moment I thought, I want to be ready to cash this check, but how?

"Think about India Arie," he says. "Think about how she sings it, how she praises her 'Brown Skin,' how she owns it."

And he starts to sing (quite beautifully) India Arie's "Brown Skin."

"I can't sing," I say.

"Don't be a smartass, you get it." He kept singing: "Skin so Brown, lips so round. Beautiful mahogany, you make me feel like a queen."

I understood what he needed from me, I did, he wanted me to sing, but not like rhythmically extending my vowels singing, no, that's singing, but what he's asking for is *SING-ING*. Like India about Brown skin, like Nina about the color of "Lilac Wine," like Aretha about the need and power of "Amazing Grace," like Roberson and that "Ol' Man River," like the first time I saw John Leguizamo's one-man show *Freak*.

Damn! That was *sing-ing*. That was praising, that was owning it. That was truly the first time I saw any resemblance of myself on a stage. I certainly hadn't seen it on TV and film. But up there, on that stage at the Cort Theatre, John Leguizamo—a Colombian kid raised in Queens, like myself—was giving me life; was making meaning of my life. I watched him in all his Brown glory on that stage. He salsa danced, he told the truth, he was confused, he was afraid, he was horny, excited, anxious, he was himself. I watched a Broadway theater full of mainly white people watching him without blinking. I watched them laughing, crying, listening, taking in every word with their hearts wide open. It was "physiological synchrony," that incredible moment when our heartbeats actually synchronize during performances (one of many reasons why theater is magic). You know, like when they say laughter is contagious? So is compassion, kindness, rage, a moment of awakening. Like when the entire audience got up at the same time in order to give him a standing ovation. It was electric, it was natural, it was pure magic. I walked out that theater feeling like (if only for a minute) I, too, was worth it.

I read somewhere that good art makes you pregnant, makes you want to birth something you didn't even know you had, and all of a sudden you must birth something into the world that feels holy, something beyond your own control or understanding, something that feels like life itself. You have no idea how it will happen, but you're positive that it must. This was the moment some sort of magical art baby was conceived in me, and I knew I had to birth it into the world.

I went home, hopped in the shower, and started imagining myself on a stage doing my very own one-man show, having no idea what it would be about, having no idea how hard my life would be in moments, no clue of all the horrible drafts, high hopes, hopes shattered, tears, bad shows, and bad breaks that would come before it.

Up until that moment, I had always been trying to find my voice, praying that I had one. I would spend hours watching TV as a kid looking for it. I would sit and watch heroes who looked nothing like me living lives I wished I could live. People who wouldn't shy away when I watched them, studied them, people who embraced my gaze as I got to know them, love them, hate them, envy them.

I watched, praying that maybe I'd see a part of myself. Any part. I was looking for my mother, my father, our community. I was searching for direction, guidance on how to act, how to live, what to say, how to say it, when, and why. I was grasping for possibilities.

At night, when my family was asleep, I would turn on the TV, sometimes with no sound at all, and I would just watch, study, and visualize being able to reach my hands inside the screen. I would grab the hero's light-skinned face, smaller features, fine and straight hair, and pull it toward me, stretching the portrait over mine. I would imagine absorbing the heroes' lives, their ease, their grace, even their ridiculous TV troubles, the adventures, the odd jobs, the ease of life, the romance, the kissing in the rain—on TV, white people are always kissing in the rain.

The TV seeped itself into my mind, drip by drip, effortlessly, until I couldn't see reality anymore. I thought, in order to be worthy of a life worth living and a story worth telling, "I have to become the boys on TV." In my mind, conscious or unconscious, I began to think that the Brown body was a symbol of less and that it was okay to not want to be Brown. I began to think it was okay to want to become something else.

And then I saw *Freak*. Now, theater was what I strived for. The theater felt like a form of activism, free from the desperation that TV constantly caused in me. The theater (although not perfect then or now) was a home (much more than the television) for both inclusion and disruption. A place that allowed you to receive story and the power of sharing that story as medicine, not just currency. Another thing to be sold.

Seeing that show at the Cort Theatre on 48th Street gave me purpose. It's why I dedicated my life from then on to the theater, to being an artist. I studied it in high school, I majored in it in college, I have traveled the world and slept on many a couch doing it.

It's quite possible that much of my voice and vision as an artist was born that day: Create art that allows others to be seen. Art that can be a vehicle for disruption, movement, and change.

I try to evoke this power and flexibility that the theater can provide when acting on a TV show, and the episode we're filming is titled "Salsa." You guessed it; it's about salsa dancing. In the opening scene, my character, the only Latin character in the show, is eating chips and salsa (convenient), and he says, and I quote, while a salsa covered chip, which his white girlfriend feeds him, is in his mouth, "Speaking of salsa, I love salsa dancing, we should go sometime." Yes, while eating salsa (the food), he is reminded of how much he also loves salsa (the dance). If you think this is funny and ridiculous, it's because it is. But wait, there's more.

My character then asks his white girlfriend to go salsa dancing with him. Which she then lies about by saying she is able to salsa dance quite well. She then goes and seeks help from her white male best friend next door, he says he has a ton of experience dancing salsa from his time in Paris (Paris!), and he decides to teach her. That proceeding scene has some Cuban salsa playing, and there is a random rose that ends up in his mouth, and it's a whole thing. After she dances with her white friend, she is super turned on by the "salsa" and decides to sleep with my character for the first time. All of that began because my character ate chips and salsa!

Here are the facts: Roses in the mouth are more tango than salsa. And I actually do love to dance salsa. I'm not bad at it either. Salsa is a big part of my life. I grew up watching my parents' perfect, quick feet glide across the floor. Talk about grace, the two of them make salsa look like the reason we all came here—to be held, to spin and be spun, to fly.

But for whatever reason, the writers must have thought it was all a little too on the nose to have the only Latin person dancing, so every character danced salsa except me.

I wanted to tell them: "Yo, this is fucked up. It's unoriginal. It's stereotypical." I wanted to inform them: "You're making fun of something incredibly special. The great *salsero* Willie Cólon said, 'Salsa was the force that united diverse Latinos. . . . Salsa is the harmonic sum of all Latin culture.' You can't celebrate salsa without recognizing that its percussion is inherited from African drums. Stolen African drums, that came over the waters with stolen African bodies. It's not just some sexy partner dance to turn you on, that you put a rose in your mouth to—again, more tango than salsa!"

I wanted to suggest: "Why don't we do the *rueda*, a Cuban group dance that is danced in a circle, with sometimes up to a hundred people? It's beautiful, your audience will love it."

I wanted to ask: "We dancing LA or NY style? Dancing on the 1 or the 2? Do you know there's a lot of drama around calling it *salsa*? The great Tito Puente, the king of timbales, said, 'The only salsa I know is sold in a bottle called ketchup. I play Cuban music.' So maybe we shouldn't talk about dancing salsa while eating salsa."

In 2020, Jimmy Kimmel said during a late-night segment, "TV is so desperate for ratings, we've had to resort to doing the right thing: inclusion." It was a joke, but like a lot of comedy, it was both funny and sad because it was true. Is this why I am a working actor? Because of Hollywood's desperation?

I didn't say anything that day. I swallowed it like I swallowed those damn chips, and I kept my mouth shut. Where was my proudness then?

I didn't say anything to them because it's scary. Because I needed the paycheck. Also, I'm not a martyr, and this isn't some sacrifice I am making. I love what I do. I am grateful to do it, grateful to be able to pay my rent doing what I love. That's what I'd always say to my pops, "Pops, I ain't trying to be Brad Pitt, just pay my rent and play ball whenever I want." It's because I love it that I can call out its obvious flaws.

That episode felt like something I genuinely loved was taken from me. Something I found in 1998 while watching John Leguizamo stand on stage singing, celebrating, and owning the fullness of his Brown being. In that moment I knew I was worth it. If only for long enough to get me to that rehearsal room in Dallas, where I was suddenly struggling to remember what that proudness felt like.

Which is funny because I created *The Real James Bond* to own that fullness and complexity proudly, to celebrate and to share that medicine with others in the way it was shared with me. Shit, it may even be why I wrote this book.

I hoped that that play was my way of saying: "Look at me, I am Latino or Latinx, I am some sort of Brown, my experience is worth it, I am not just another cog in the wheel. I belong here."

Desmond Tutu once said, "Every person wants to be acknowledged and affirmed for who and what they are, a human being of infinite worth, someone with a place in the world."

I believe that's why we (and most definitely I) do everything and anything we do, to be acknowledged and affirmed for who we are. That is especially why we tell stories, make theater, art, write, sing, dance, share, tour the country, hit up open mics and friend's backyards, travel the world—to reveal ourselves, to share our truths, to share these knowings and unknowings, to say, "What you're dreaming about, what you aspire to be, it's possible!" So that one tiny universe (mine) can meet another tiny universe (yours), and together we make a third tiny universe (this experience), so we can get free, so we can have a grand moment of physiological synchrony. Brown people coming into their truth and being fully congruent with who they are all at once. So we can *sing*!

Again, not the extended vowels singing. No, this is more from the heart, about the heart, about the life in-between, behind, underneath, around, and over the words. It's the *duende* that the great Spanish playwright and poet Federico García Lopez talked about: *duende* is the spirit of the artist in their finest moments, a visiting spirit that takes you over and will only come to you when you are open and authentic. I choose *duende*, I choose to open up my ribs so that I can sing all the shades of pain, worth, worship, beauty, and truth that come with my Brown skin.

I don't *have* to sing; I *get* to sing. I get to share, because I wrote these words into existence, and words are powerful. The words we speak can create love, happiness, trust, they can set us free, or they can create a perpetual hell. The Tony Award–winning playwright Suzan-Lori Parks says, "Words are spells in your mouth." Okay. Then, what words am I speaking? What spells am I putting into the earth? Do I have the courage to speak and write words about situations of social injustice, even when doing so may threaten my own safety?

I've seen *Harry Potter*, I've watched *Charmed*, I know that in magic one wrong word can cast something else entirely, one breath changes the whole thing. Must I love myself first, have self-worth first, or can I speak it all into existence? Can I say it if I don't know it, if it hasn't settled into my body yet? Can I use my art as a platform to become who I want to be? Or must I be that thing first in order to say the words, "Proudly, in my own Brown Skin?"

But there is a second very important half to that Suzan-Lori Parks quote: "You speak in order to change something in the world." That's right. What do I want to change in this world? More importantly, am I ready? Are my words ready? Is my mouth ready? If I speak the wrong words do I make the wrong change? Am I ready to be proud on that stage and speak my truth?

I think so, I hope so, I really do . . .

A great mentor of mine (who has now passed) named Laurie Carlos, a fabulous theater director who worked with the "jazz aesthetic," whenever I was obsessed with getting a thing right, would always remind me: "Chris, it's not your job to figure it out. It's not your job to get it right. It's your job to say the words, and then maybe six, seven years from now you'll be grabbing groceries and suddenly it'll hit you—BOOM. You just have to keep moving forward."

Keep moving forward. It's not about solving all of the world's problems with my spell. It's not about having the perfect plan in place before I begin, I just have to begin. I don't have to fix the whole tree, because sometimes nourishing the soil, the water, the things around it, or just a single leaf can do a lot of good.

In the years of touring *The Real James Bond* around the country, where we have engaged in countless post-show story circles, I've witnessed audience members in public spaces saying things they have never said out loud to a room full of strangers. When I perform this show and I speak my truth without trying to get it right, when I sing, however I can sing that day, when I trust the words, the spells, great change happens.

Like the white man married to an Afro-Latino woman who confessed: "My love, I'm sorry. I thought I was aware, and I am shocked and horrified at how little I have paid attention to what is really happening. I'm sorry."

There was the young Brown boy studying theater at Pace University. He came up to me after the show and said: "I always thought I needed heroes that looked like me, stars, and epic stories, but after seeing you, I now know that what I need is normal people, normal stories, normal beautiful Brownness just being us. I just need people like me. Thank you for being you."

We end every show and story circle with the same question, "What is one thing or one more thing that you can do daily to work toward ending racism, bias, hate, oppression, and violence, and to make the world a better place for all people?"

Imagine if everyone reading this began doing just that one thing. That's a lot of individual leaves that can begin to communally nourish a very sick tree. You and I are the leaves, the soil, and the air that can nourish the plant. Right here, right now, as we are.

Words *are* spells in our mouths, and we must speak in order to change something. No more waiting. I'm casting a big fat spell, right here, right now. A spell where every word matters, every word sets us free a little more, brings us together a little more, heals a little more. An anti-invisibility spell, a spell of self-worth, for myself and the other Brown girls and boys who need to see themselves grander and more vibrant but who don't, a spell that says, "I get it, I see you, you are not alone."

The Water We Swim In

"If you stick a knife in my back nine inches and pull it out six inches, there's no progress. If you pull it all the way out, that's not progress. Progress is healing the wound that the blow made. And they haven't even begun to pull the knife out, much less heal the wound. They won't even admit the knife is there."

—MALCOLM X

ONE.

"It is amazing the weapons people disguise as small talk," a friend says. I had just told her about a recent experience I had at a photoshoot for a new TV show in which I was just cast.

"And they have no idea what they're firing out of that weapon," I said.

"None."

It was a normal shoot, as shoots go. Camera snapping. Outfit changes. The photographer and I were talking, small talk, and then he asked: "You seeing someone? Got a lady?"

I wondered why he assumed it was a she. "I do," I said.

"Oh, so, your girl's Latin, yeah?"

He assumed, likely because I, too, am Latin. "She is," I said.

"Oooohhh, she spicy?" he asked.

"Spicy," this motherfucker said "spicy." Like I date a food. Like I date a flavor. Like I date a TV character, a hypersexualized and oftentimes degraded "Spicy Latina." Like all Latin American and Spanish speaking countries are filled with Sofia Vergara's character from *Modern Family*. They're not. But that's the thing because it's not completely his fault. Eva Longoria is often "spicy." J. Lo can be "spicy." Images of Latin women in media are often spicy.

My friend, a Latina herself who has been referred to as "spicy," called it "fucked up microaggressions."

Except I don't like that term because there is really nothing micro about them at all.

"Yo," I said to the photographer, "first of all, you can't just open your mouth all willy-nilly, you can't just think that everything the media shoves down your throat is what is, you can't go around calling Latin women spicy—"

He cut me off and said, "No, it's not like that, I used to date a Colombian woman, I was just being funny."

I continued, "Two, just because you once dated a Brown person doesn't mean what you're saying is okay, that's like saying you have Black friends. You dating a Latin woman does not give us shared intimacy.

"Three, my lady would likely smack you across the face if she heard you refer to her as spicy, and that would suck, for her, for your face, but mainly because then you actually would think she's spicy. It's a real lose-lose situation. You feel me?"

I was waiting for some sort of quick retort from the photographer. But he said nothing, and his assistants looked away, one of them hid her face behind the bounce board.

"We almost done here?" I asked.

My story is not singular. In fact, when it comes to the bullshit that bodies of color have to put up with on a daily basis, it is par for the course. Or as Resmaa Menakem says, "Bodies of culture."

I love "bodies of culture" way more, because it reminds me of what is lost in the many nuances of assimilation and making white people comfortable. It is part of moving toward a predominantly white ideal of "success." It is even more common that bodies of culture are pushed and tested to a point where they must determine whether opening their mouths to speak up for common human dignity is harmful to their survival.

I'm almost positive that this includes people like Sofia Vergara or Eva Longoria or J. Lo, who have the additional burdens of dealing with the inherent misogyny that's tied to being a successful "spicy" woman. Imagine the daily aggressions they have encountered in their movement toward success.

I have been on many TV sets where some misogynistic or racist comment is uttered and the room just goes quiet, but I don't say anything because I don't have the freedom to say anything, I can't afford to lose my job.

Who will speak up for us, so we don't have to keep fighting on our own behalf? Who will call people on their shit? Like why didn't the other six people in the room say something about that comment, about the many comments I'm sure he has made in the past?

These aggressions are happening everywhere and all the time, it's ever-present. We just need others to take notice.

TWO.

The other night I was invited to this small, intimate, bougie dinner in Venice, California, by a very well-known, publicly "woke," bestselling author and meditation teacher. We had connected a few nights before at an event where I was giving a talk. She and her husband came up to me after and said they were throwing this dinner and that they'd love me to join. I am more of a "yes" than a "no" person, but also these people looked like the kind of folks who on any given night throw a great dinner party, a cult indoctrination, an orgy, or a candlelit event where someone is sacrificed . . . so, I said sure.

A week later, I walked into their home in Venice, and my skin started to crawl. The home was trying too hard, way too hard. For one, there was an open concept rain shower in their living room—with a glass bottom and top so you could be seen from both sides. I am not against nudity, I never wear a shirt, and I rarely wear pants at home, but your shower doesn't need to be in your living room, just getting water everywhere. There were large sculptures ubiquitously placed willy-nilly and the dining room table had these very large uncomfortable black boxes for seats—I don't care how much money you have, a seat should be more comfortable than artistic, and if it is gonna be art, make it comfortable art.

I wasn't in the house for more than two minutes when they said, "This house had a scene in *Point Break*."

"Oh . . . cool," I replied.

The older I get, the more difficult it is to engage in small talk or pretend that I like something or am impressed when I'm not.

But worse than the décor was the lack of diversity. I've also realized that the older I get, the more difficult it is to act like I comfortably fit in a room full of only white bodies.

Right before we sat down to dinner, a tall and beautiful Black woman walked in and apologized for being late. Her name was Alice, and I breathed a deeper breath than I'd breathed all night, and thought: "Tight, maybe I won't get murdered? Or, they needed one boy and one girl to sacrifice? Balance. At least I won't go out alone."

Alice and I locked eyes at the pace in which the only two non-white people in a room lock eyes—fast.

Our hosts for the evening ordered Café Gratitude for us, a vegan restaurant where all the food is called some sort of affirmation, which they make you say when you order (i.e., "Can I please have the 'I am magnificent' and also the 'I am restored,' and she'll have the 'I am magical'?"). But the food is yummy, so no issue there.

We're sitting down, and everything is pleasant. The host has table games, ways to spark conversation and introduce one another. I can't tell you what led to this next comment, but our woke host who travels the world teaching mindfulness said the words "I don't believe anyone is more privileged than anyone else."

FUCK!

I just wanted to have dinner. I just wanted to eat this food and make boring small talk and go home and tell my friends about this very white dinner I just attended, but now, now I gotta deal with this shit.

Again, as fast as the only two people of color can make eye contact in a room, Alice and I made contact, *fast*.

I know we were both thinking the same things: "Who's gonna speak up? Should I? Will you? Do we have to? Why do we have to? Will someone else? What the fuck? Why were we invited to this? I was just trying to eat. Is it rude to take food to go? Maybe I let this one pass? Now I gotta go and ruin the night and make it all awkward at this weird and uncomfortable postmodern table."

I knew one of us had to say something, but I didn't want Alice to bear the burden, so I responded: "Excuse me, but you inherited wealth and privilege the moment bodies were stolen from their homes in order to give you this wealth, this food, this street corner, everything we stand on. You inherited privilege when someone made up that it was better to be poor and white rather than poor and Black. You can write all the books and do all the meditations, retreats, and give all the talks, but your body and your cells aren't around long enough for you to comprehend the bloodshed, trauma, and abuse that lets you stand here in all this privilege."

I'm not really sure why it came out like a planned dissertation. I wasn't seeking to expend some sort of emotional labor. Sometimes the words used in ignorance and privilege hurt, and I guess I just don't want to be hurt anymore.

And then it got weird and awkward and quiet, a heavy, thick, full, knife through the butter quiet. Everyone was waiting for something or someone else to save the moment. I love it when you can feel the weight of time. When the clock is slower than it's been, like it's sitting on top of a hot stove.

Our host avoided eye contact with me at all costs. She tried to save herself with the classic line, "That's not what I meant."

"What did you mean?" I asked.

The husband stepped in and tried to take the energy away from her. "Look, it's a misunderstanding and I think we need to let it breathe."

"We've been letting racism breathe for centuries, but, sure, let's let it breathe," I said.

The next thirty-nine minutes were an attempt to support, not escalate, and maintain some sort of chill environment, aka real small small-talk. And right before it looked like we could all escape this thing before people were crying, Alice spoke up and said: "It's exhausting to teach. You know that, right? Why did you say that? And why did none of you correct her? It's draining. You should be ashamed of yourselves. All of you. It's not enough that we have to walk around constantly trying to grasp our own worth, no, now we have to teach you, too! You write books, you have voices, use them!"

Austin Channing Brown says that the "role of a bridge builder sounds appealing, until you realize the bridge has your broken back."

Homegirl across from me was done building bridges. Done. She thanked everyone and bounced.

I thought about leaving with her, solidarity and whatnot, but also I'm kind of a glutton for awkward situations. I was pretty excited by how uncomfortable they would be with one of us hanging around. I was curious how much they would kiss my ass. The answer—*a lot.*

They were sweet, but they certainty lacked the tools to talk about it, to engage in it, to be real about it, to sit in it, to unearth it, to not try to solve it or cover it up, just to be with the ugliness of it all. Throughout the rest of the evening, each guest (the husband included) took me to the side individually and lowered their voice as if solidarity and doing the right thing should be a secret, all saying something along the lines of "That was fucked up. I'm sorry. That's not okay."

Each time I replied in a normal volume, not secret volume, "Okay, well next time say this out loud so we don't have to."

I spent the rest of that evening experiencing the other guests feeling very uncomfortable. It was nice, real nice. I used to think that whenever racial tension arose, I must be the problem, but I now know I am not. I now know that tension is a good thing. Most white people don't experience enough of the repercussions of sitting in the shit that comes out of their mouths. The premise that whiteness is supreme, better, best, permeates the air we breathe—it's in our schools, in our offices, at our dinner parties, and in our country. It makes the feelings of whiteness (which is really just a steady feeling of power and comfort) the most important thing. And more often, they need to know it's not important, how white people feel is less important than how they make other people feel with what they say and do.

A couple weeks later, the host reached out to me, she wanted to grab coffee and apologize. She figured we'd run into each other soon enough; we do share the same book agent after all.

"I'm really sorry about the other night," she said.

"Look, the one thing I'm still caught up on is, if you can get flown all over the world to speak and to teach to sold-out crowds of thousands of people, and your belief system is one of 'I don't believe anyone is more privileged than anyone else,' then what are we as a society promoting, accepting, allowing, and teaching?" I asked.

"You're right. Part of my practice is acknowledging when I'm wrong."

"I don't care that I am right. Honestly, the part that keeps me awake is, if I don't accept that rhetoric, which I don't, if I fight against it, which I do, will that hinder my ability to be successful?"

In some circles, it just might. Really, it might. But fuck those circles, I don't care to pretend anymore.

THREE.

I was performing a play in New England, where we talk about the death of a ten-year-old boy named Lonnie Wesson, who was hit by a stray bullet in a drive-by in Miami. One of many ten-year-olds, of many boys and girls who are killed every day, in and out of Miami.

When the show was over, a little fourth grader, a boy from a fancy Montessori school with a tuition of thirty-thousand dollars a year (I know because I looked it up) asked me if the little boy in the play actually got killed, if he was actually shot.

I responded without hesitation, "Yes."

He asked, "Does that still happen?"

Immediately, I said, "Yes, every day."

He asked, "Today?"

I said, "Yeah, possibly, probably."

He asked, "Where?"

I told him, "Everywhere."

That boy's eyes got as wide as any eyes I'd ever seen. My castmates gave me shit for not having a little more tact. "Be gentle, Chris," they said.

Gentle? Boy's got to grow up and see what's going on around here. Now is as good a time as ever. I prayed that the moment he goes home and asks his white parents about the little boys and girls being shot every day, wondering, "Mommy, Daddy, is it true?" that they tell him, "Yes."

But I don't know that they did. If he brought it up, what did they say to him? How far did they go to ease his wounds, to protect his bubble, to protect the lie that everything is fine?

Or did they actually grab their child's head and sink it deep into the water, drowning him in the truth? Did they say, "Yes, yes son, every day, everywhere, little, big, and medium Brown and Black boys and girls are being shot, harassed, profiled, choked, suffocated, weaponized, and are born running on a treadmill with a target on their back. And no, it's not fair. Yes, son, yes, it's true."

I didn't hold back from responding to that boy because my ancestors have been holding back for centuries. I didn't hold back because look where saying the right thing has gotten us. I didn't hold back because doing the emotional labor and work is fucking exhausting, and it isn't mine to do alone. The burden of change has been placed on the ones who have needed others to change for far too long. Not anymore.

I want ease, rest, support, and softness. I want my people to do less work. I want a white fourth grader in New England to also begin to do the work with me.

I don't think that is a crazy request.

This is how we begin to change things from the very beginning. It must begin early. We must rewrite the narrative of what it means to be accountable and step up early for others.

FOUR.

When I was twenty-four, I had no permanent home for a year. I was living in LA, sleeping in my car. I was working multiple jobs, three jobs actually, and sometimes babysitting; it just wasn't enough to be enough. I had to pay my student loans, so that they wouldn't call my parents, so they wouldn't know I was struggling. I got gas for my car, lived on food stamps, and housing became low on my list of priorities. In that year I did have some pretty unbelievable luck getting housesitting gigs, but mainly I slept in my car.

Then one day, somehow, someway, I got approved for a credit card. My first credit card. I knew immediately that my first purchase was going to be a hotel room for the night. Fuck it, I deserved it. You know how hard it is to sleep in your car? Newsflash: people without shelter are not lazy.

I downloaded the Hotel Tonight app. I had been dreaming about the moment I could afford a hotel for the night. I picked a spot, and I remember it was exactly $190, which seemed expensive for a very average quality hotel that didn't even include a continental breakfast.

I spent the night. I slept really well. I took a long shower, multiple times. I left.

The other day I was leaving my current apartment, and I was driving down Sunset Boulevard, a street I've driven down a thousand times, and I looked to my left and said: "Damn, that's it. That's the hotel."

I now live 0.4 miles away from that hotel. I can walk there in thirteen minutes.

That whole time, that whole year, no one knew I was without a permanent home and sleeping in my car. No one knew. Why? A million reasons: to keep up appearances, to not be a public failure, to not worry others, to lie to myself, to grind it out, to persevere, to not have to come to terms with it, to not be weak. Most of all I was afraid what people would think of me, and what people thought of me was everything.

That is possibly the biggest microaggression of all, the one I have often perpetuated against myself in order to keep up appearances. An indirect, subtle, discrimination against my marginalized self.

For so long I wanted to be seen not as myself, not as my circumstances, not as my struggles, not as my features. I wanted to be other than myself. I believe these microaggressions against ourselves (marginalized bodies) are taking place daily because society has told us not to be ourselves, to be other than ourselves. To be successful. So, we do whatever we can, and take the shots and take the cuts and aggressions in hopes of that success.

As I write this at 12:24 a.m. in Los Angeles, in the fall of 2021, something feels clear in me—I'm tired. I was tired then, and I am tired now. Tired of trying to get it right, of trying to be enough for whiteness, trying to be seen by whiteness, loved by whiteness, accepted by whiteness, not murdered by whiteness. I am tired of caring what whiteness thinks. It doesn't care about me. At times it thinks it does, but it doesn't. Or else whiteness would step up and out in front of injustice, would step in *front* of our weaponized bodies, whiteness wouldn't stand for the "microaggressions" anymore, whiteness would save the drowning, because this "microaggression" is not micro at all. It's in the water in which we were all born and swimming daily, and each and every one of us is drowning in it, because the water is poisoned, like the fish in a plastic-filled ocean. The meditation teacher at dinner is drowning, the guests are drowning, the child in Connecticut is drowning, his parents are drowning, even the woke people are drowning, the celebrities, the doctors, the scholars, we are all drowning. And how many of us are standing by idle, watching it happen?

Did you know there are algorithms to stop nudity on Instagram and Twitter and all these ways to shut misinformation about vaccines down immediately, but there isn't an algorithm for all the racist shit that gets said on social media every other minute? Interesting. Makes me think that everything outside of these aggressions is maybe really just micro-dignity, micro-humanity, micro-equal rights.

I think part of what makes the water we're all swimming in so hostile is that we are so desperate to keep ourselves afloat that we can't see when we're pushing someone else down below us.

But what if every once in a while we just stopped and we looked around? What if we saw each other, the social refugees, or disenfranchised and downtrodden, or actual physical I-have-no-home-to-return-to refugees, or the without shelter person on my block, around my blocks, the friend in need, the person asking for help, anyone, my barista, or the cashier lady at the grocery store whose name I never remember?

What if I stopped trying to prevent my own death for long enough to see beyond my own life? Because with that sight, maybe, hopefully, we can stop each other from drowning.

Please Don't Hate Me for Dating White Women

"As far as I knew white women were never lonely, except in books. White men adored them, Black men desired them, and Black women worked for them."

—MAYA ANGELOU

Over the years I have dated Brown women and Black women, but mostly a lot of white women.

The story I began to sell myself early on, starting back in high school, was I'm not white, I'm not Black, and oftentimes in my neighborhood I wasn't Latin enough for any Latin girl I was trying to kick it to. For whatever reason, they weren't having it. I legit wasn't Brown enough—but for the white girls, I was the bee's knees.

Somewhere along the way, I picked up the belief that I was made for white women. My friends would call me "the white girl whisperer." They'd sit around in circles talking smack: "I never hooked up with a white girl, I gotta do that," or, "You're the type of Brown guy white girls like." They'd joke, "I'm about to be like you Chris and find me a white girl." As if I'd achieved something, as if I'd done us all right, reached the pinnacle, climbed the mountain, and found the Holy Grail (insert choir singing that angelic heavenly hymn) known as white women.

Yes, white women, in my mind, consciously or unconsciously, were the Holy Grail. I'm not alone. For centuries, they've played that role. Sigmund Freud himself once said, "Europeans were driven by power and sex." No surprise. Europeans set up the world's first whorehouses, kinky art shows, live sex exhibitions, and magazines with every sexual act imaginable. European men also fetishized women of color, but at the forefront of this "power and sex" was the image of the white woman.

Although times are slowly changing, the story often still remains the same. Television, movies, billboards, magazines, and four thousand Instagram ads a day still paint white women as the most coveted prize on earth. White women are viewed as upwardly mobile, multifaceted, multitasking entities who always know what to do in any situation. They are fun, beautiful, free-spirited, photogenic, easy to travel with, and you should definitely find a way to be with them or, at the very least, buy what they are selling.

When I was a kid, I would watch my pops get ready in the morning, prepping his mask for the day. I would study each and every move. It was a masterful work of art: first, it was a fresh shave, followed by a ton of cologne (he's Dominican, so it's important that you know he's coming, and that you know he's there), and then blow-drying his hair to get the perfect coif before delicately taking a Black sharpie to any stray grays that might pop up in his goatee. He took longer to get ready than my mother and sister combined. I'd sit on the toilet and ask him: "Why, Pops? What's it all for?"

My pops would tell me about how as a young man in the Dominican Republic, you had to work hard perfecting yourself, preparing your mask, so that when a young European or American woman came through, she might "choose you," as he would put it, taking you home with her, like that was your only way out.

Later, my pops made his way to New York City, where he met my mother, who is a beautiful, light-skinned, white-passing Colombian. He no longer had to perfect himself, he no longer had to be "chosen." But that morning and every morning after, and to this day, he kept up his morning ritual because old habits are hard to break.

From those conversations, I learned how I don't feel like myself without something that makes me desirable to people I don't know. I learned how important it was to be "chosen," selected. But selected by whom became and remains my dilemma. On one hand, it was an honor to be chosen by white women, and on the other hand, I felt subtly like a possession.

The first time a white woman touched me inappropriately, I was just a boy. She came in for a kiss on the cheek, and somehow it ended up on my lips (oops). I didn't say anything. And yet, this cheek-lip thing with white women has happened more times than I can count.

I used to tell myself it was cool. I was Antonio Banderas in his prime. I was Javier Bardem in *Vicky Cristina Barcelona*. I was chosen, fulfilling my purpose, or some shit like that. I was seen and desired, and I played my part of the Latin lover to perfection. My body and curls were theirs in exchange for a compliment, or even just a smiling glance.

I thought I was being treated with respect. I thought I was being accepted. And as a young Brown kid, that's one of the things I wanted most: to fit into the world as though I belonged. I thought by dating white women I could become *white enough* to belong.

The first time I slept with a white woman, I wore it like a badge of honor. I went home thinking: "I am worthy. I am beautiful." It was like an affirmation from the universe.

All through high school and college, I dated white women and thought nothing of it. I thought nothing of it when I went to my girlfriend's house after dating her for eight months to finally meet her parents. I sat down at the dinner table and her mom asked, "What's PR like?"

"PR?" I asked.

"Puerto Rico."

"Oh. I don't know. I've never been. I hear it's nice."

Her dad chimed in: "You've never been. Wow. Surprising. Do you still have family there?"

"No, um, I'm not Puerto Rican. I'm Dominican and Colombian."

Everyone awkwardly looked at my girlfriend as I asked: "Did you tell them I was Puerto Rican? We've been together for eight months."

In order to save the situation, the mother interjected, "*Buena Vista Social Club* was a really great film."

I thought nothing of it when I went over to a white girl's house for dinner and her father opened the door and said, "Sorry, tonight's not taco night," and then closed the door in my face, only to open it again because he was "just joking."

I stayed for a flavorless casserole.

I thought nothing of it when a white woman I was briefly seeing made several borderline offensive comments while we were flirting: "What will your parents think if you bring a white girl home? When you tell your friends about us? They'll think you got quite a catch, won't they?"

I chose to ignore it, maybe because she was right. I did think I'd landed myself quite a catch—a white girl.

I thought nothing of it when a half-naked bubbly white girl asked while straddling me, "Do you speak Mexican?"

Time froze. I wanted her to know that it was Spanish, that Mexican isn't a language. I wanted her to know that I actually speak Spanish pretty badly, but I didn't want the straddling part to end, and I chose sex over dignity. I didn't know how to say no to a white woman's gaze or touch. Who would I become if I stopped playing this part of the Latin lover? Would I still be invited? Would I still have worth? Would I still be me?

I was so deep into the illusion that I thought I might crumble without it.

And though they were always there, I started to actually hear the people in my community giving me a hard time, friends and family and their sly off-hand jokes: "There he goes again with a white girl. He couldn't actually handle a girl of color, they wouldn't put up with his shit. Chris says he's Latin, but he's too afraid to actually date one."

Whether in nonwhite spaces or in absolutely all-white spaces, I started to see the looks and glances. It felt like daggers coming from people's eyes, watching me like I was doing something wrong, as if they would be happier if I just stopped dating white women, as if they thought Black and Brown people would somehow be better off if I—Christopher William Rivas—dumped my white girlfriend. It became a lot of pressure.

The world seemed to be whispering: "Pick a side, Chris. Pick a side."

I could no longer look at my white girlfriend without asking myself, *Why do I date so many white women? Is it because I like them or because I think I should like them?*

In today's hashtag-woke society, there is mad pressure to be hashtag-woke—to be aware of the implications of to whom I am attracted and why. Which means that in the eyes of others, the color of the women I date is a big deal. Like I'm betraying my people if I date white women. Like I'm the problem.

Even if I was taught that we were all one people.

So, I went searching for answers. I started reading James Baldwin and Eldridge Cleaver. I turned to other authors of culture looking for guidance, a roadmap, help on what it means to be a Brown man in the world. Like, yes, our bodies have been colonized. Yes, I am a child of Blackness. Yes, the body of color has done more for society than it has gotten in return. Yes, society seems to want to embrace a *lot* of things associated with the culture of color without actually being a person of color.

White people worship Beyoncé and yet they killed Breonna Taylor.

Meanwhile, I am contemplating my entire dating history and its role in civilization. Gabi, my white girlfriend, has no idea because I don't actually share that I'm having a racial breakdown. Instead, I tell her: "I need a break. I need to find myself. I need to do me for a while."

"But everything is good," Gabi replied with that sad hopefulness I've come to expect in my relationships.

"Yeah, it is," I declared. "But I just feel like I need to be alone. I haven't done that in a long time."

She could see right through my shit: "Bullshit, Chris. What are you lying about? What aren't you telling me?"

I could see the tears coming, this could be the moment I tackle and conquer this inability to communicate head-on. I could come clean and say how I really feel. Instead I fail: "Nothing. I promise. It's . . . it's nothing. I just need space. Sorry."

Am I the problem or is it everyone else? If everyone is so woke, why are things so terrible? How do I love in a Brown body in a way that makes everybody happy? Am I woke enough to no longer suffer from white skin fetishism, which is the product of colonialism and patriarchy? Or am I specifically focused on feedback from white women for the same reason?

I fell for a white woman, and she fell for me—simple as that—yet I feel as if I'm doing the wrong thing by dating her. Despite how much I have felt like we are falling in love, or how much fun we have, I'm also tired of constantly evaluating myself through a white lens, subjecting myself to white standards. I am tired of hating on myself.

Because even in this relationship that feels so warm and normal, I can't help but wonder, do white women find me attractive or do they see me as some exotic idea they should find attractive? Do I find white women attractive, or do I see them as some exotic idea I should find attractive? Do I even know to whom I'm attracted or why?

I tell a buddy afterwards, "My body has been colonized, and so I probably shouldn't date white women for a while until I decolonize."

"You're so dramatic, Rivas," he replied.

"I'll be the first to agree with you, but for as far as back as I can remember, I've been brainwashed by the idea that the hand I hold has more value than my own."

Like my pops said, "Maybe they'll choose you."

"Maybe they'll choose you" is a message amplified by movies and TV old and new. We like to believe that our dating tendencies are organic and unbiased, but a great deal of our preferences stem from the images and media we consume and their ideas (the storytellers and execs) about beauty standards, whether that be character traits or physical attributes. How much of our dating choices and attractions are learned rather than an honest biological reality?

From *Save the Last Dance*, *The Big Sick*, *Master of None*, and *The Great White Hope* (where the white woman is literally the "hope") to *La Bamba* among dozens of other narratives, the story is the same: a Black or Brown man is made better, in some cases is even saved, by being with a white woman.

Just see the work of Kumail Nanjiani and Aziz Ansari, where consistent overt as well as subliminal messaging is "get a white woman, and your problems will be solved." Your life will get better. Except *Get Out*, which is what I felt like I needed to do.

Remember how I talked about the show *Woke*? Well, at the beginning of the series, he breaks up with his Black girlfriend who isn't woke enough (I infer), and somehow by the end of the series, our now *Woke* hero ends up dating a white woman. Not saying it's bad, just a funny coincidence.

I brought home a Black girl in high school, and my *tía* angrily mumbled from the kitchen, "Ay, do you see him and that Negrita?"

I should have spoken up: "Ay, yo, stop! You ever look at your own family albums? You ever look at me? You ever look at yourself? We ain't white. Not even close."

But I didn't say anything. *Pick a side, Chris. Pick a goddamn side.*

Since I lacked the ability to tell my partner what was actually going on, I decided instead to write a scene about it for my play *The Real James Bond . . . Was Dominican!*

The scene was a hit; after every show, people would thank me for it. They laughed, they cried, they wondered why they too dated so many white people.

When I asked my Korean-American friend about her preference for white men, she admitted, "I haven't really thought about it."

"Really?" I asked.

"All my other Korean friends dated white guys, it just seemed like the norm. I guess if I really dig in, maybe I've only dated white men because I imagine that I want my children to have the privilege and status I still don't have."

My buddy who's Black and married to a Black woman has a different take: "There is something about coming home and knowing that she knows, she just knows the struggle, the ridiculousness, the beauty and plight of being a body of color . . . There is no educating, Chris. Sometimes we don't even have to say anything or talk about it. She just knows. She gets me."

When he said that, I felt a peace I could rarely find in my relationships. I wanted someone who just *gets me.* Don't we all? Often when dating white women, I wouldn't even tell them about my experiences as a Brown man. Shit (big and small) would happen as I was heading over to their apartment, and I never said a word. Minorities live in a racist society every day. There's already a lot of heavy lifting that bodies of color are doing. Having to explain the experience just compounds the trauma. It is sometimes nice to date someone who just gets it. Assuming they get it. Which is not a guarantee for anyone, melanin or not.

I still hadn't told my ex about any of this—I know, I know. As if the scene in a publicly touring show around the country wasn't enough, I then submitted an article to the "Modern Love" section of the *New York Times.*

It was originally titled "Please Don't Hate Me for Dating White Women," but they sensationalized the headline, turning it into "I Broke Up with Her Because She's White." The article went massively viral and was translated into six different languages.

I got thousands of emails, a mix of hate and confessions, fury and rage. The article was picked up and spread around by a white supremacist with more than a million followers on YouTube, because in 2019, everyone can and likely does have a platform. I was a symbol for "woke racism," which apparently means you are a bullseye for hate mail. I was called a "coon," an "Aztec warrior piece of shit," the N-word by a lot of folks, and I was compared to Jim Crow, which is really intense. I was called "spick swine" more than once, though I'm not sure what pigs have to do with all this. And I quickly learned that the favorite word of white "woke" people is "bigot." I thought, I'm just trying to be real here, but being real costs a lot.

I read them all (I do *not* advise this). I saved them all (also not advised).

Though the offenses were numerous, the confessions cut even deeper. Confessions like, "I once called someone the N-word." Or, "My parents won't let me date a Black man." Or, "This is how I feel when I date Brown men." One of the most common themes was: "I'm dating a white woman who has no other people of color in her life, no other Latinos, maybe one Black friend. And now, I'm beginning to think that is an issue. I can't be the only person of color in her life . . . right?"

None of them were healing to my soul, because bearing all the weight of people's confessions and questions about what's right and wrong, about their feelings, and what they should do is heavy emotional lifting. None of them considered how they might affect the person receiving them.

At least the blatantly hateful ones have a clear intention— they want to hurt me. But the confessions are seeking something far more deceitful, they want me to tell them it's okay. They want me to give them a free pass and absolution. They want me to make them feel better.

I never responded to any of them, but then again, I hadn't even responded to my ex yet.

Oh yeah, that. Because outside of the dark hole that is internet trolls, I had also fallen deeper into my ego. See, as much as I was reviled in some circles, I was being revered in others. Overnight, I was launched into this role of "the voice of Brownness." Which was fine. Someone has to do it, why not me? I was offered a TV writing job, book agents were calling left and right, I was interviewed for radio shows, podcasts, and magazines. It was overwhelming, especially since all I was trying to do was honor my experience, express my voice, and have the courage to stand up and say: "This shit is confusing. Here is my experience as a Brown body."

But like the emails asking for absolution, I was ignoring the person to whom the article was directed. Soon after it came out, all of my friends were texting and calling me, asking: "Have you spoken to Gabi about this? You should probably give her a call."

I knew she read the article, and I knew she knew it was about her. I knew my public self-exploration and burgeoning "success" came at her public expense.

Finally, we met in a park.

"People know me," Gabi said, her voice filled with hurt.

"I know," I sheepishly responded.

"They know us. My family—"

I cut her off, "I'm sorry."

But she wouldn't let me. "Fuck you! Jesus, Chris, I mean, I'm happy for you but—"

"I'm sorry," I tried again.

"Shut up," she looked down. "Let me talk. I'm happy for you, okay? I am. You just, you should have said something to me about this. You vanished. You had so many chances to tell me. And this is how you do it? You humiliate me?"

"Look, they rewrote the title, and that's fucked up, because this title sucks."

She began to shake her head as I continued, grasping at why my search for identity had become a betrayal of intimacy. "Also, it's an examination, not a declaration."

She got up to leave as I called to her: "Gabi, wait. I do care for you. I don't know why I didn't say anything . . . I couldn't . . . There is a lot of stuff inside, and it just came pouring out all at once."

But she didn't look back. I stood wondering if my tendency to confess things publicly was serving anyone.

I tell myself it's courage, a way of facing my demons head-on. I call it vulnerability and being authentic. I am a storyteller for a living, sharing my confessions with hundreds and thousands of people. And yet, when I'm mano a mano, I can't say shit.

I think I'm being vulnerable, but my therapist disagrees. I sit across from him a week after meeting Gabi in the park, like I'm in some Latinx version of a Woody Allen movie but without the creepy backstory. He listens to me because that's what he's paid to do, but then he earns the insurance copay, telling me: "There is no risk in storytelling, Chris. You're just reading something you wrote, prepared to share it. You can't prepare for intimacy and vulnerability. That's the shit that really hurts. That's showing someone who you truly are."

Every week, I think this will be my last session. Every week, I think I have my shit together enough not to return. I mean, he spends half the time yawning, seriously. I know it's super early, 8 a.m. on Mondays, but still, it's kind of rude. Anyway, he always seems to say one thing that stops me in my tracks, like "You can't prepare for intimacy and vulnerability. That's the shit that really hurts. That's showing someone who you truly are."

I used to think intimacy was about sex, bedroom, clothes-off stuff. But recently during my meditation practice I've been thinking about what it means to be intimate with everything, or as my meditation teacher says, to "let the heat kill you." Meaning whatever it is, we experience it fully. Boredom, experience it fully. Doubt, confusion, experience it. We don't take a lot of time to experience something to its full potential. That takes showing up with enough courage and presence to be intimate with your own life and everything that comes with it. Intimate enough to show someone (myself included) the truth, what I know, what I don't know, what I'm afraid of, struggling with, and the things I can't yet communicate. Part of that intimacy is the conversation about race, pain, and trauma. It can be uncomfortable. But intimacy isn't just rainbows, it's also the muck and being willing to sit in the muck, sometimes with another person, sitting with all of it, in all of it.

Let the heat kill you.

I have dated women of color since Gabi, and it's been equally nice and equally challenging. A person of color was not a magic pill for the things I lacked. Yes, there were moments where two bodies of color can look at each other, smile, and at the same exact time, say, "Oh, white people." Those moments are fun, but the struggles still remain. If anything, there are plenty of white people who are aware enough to also share that same sentiment, "Oh, white people."

Because wokeness can become its own burden, forcing people of culture to run everything through the filter of race. As unwoke as it might sound, the kind of intimacy I am seeking goes way beyond skin color. Now I can confidently say, I won't date white women. I'll date a human who is having a vibrant living dialogue with their own identity. Someone who sees where I am and wants to meet me there. And I need to be willing to do the same for them.

So here I stand, trying to be properly woke, Brown, intimate, courageous, Latinx, asking a lot of questions, decolonizing, and investigating my desire, yearning, praying, journaling, writing, dialoguing, putting up a one-man show, writing a book, wishing, trying to wrap my head and heart around this, and hoping I'm doing okay.

Because there are things in us that can *only* blossom with another person, things that will never be unearthed without them. If I run to examine it alone every time, I'll just end up deeper in ego and further away from intimacy, cut off from some of the best shit life has to offer. If I keep running, I won't ever get that moment that my friend talked about, where I soften and let my guard down enough for someone to get me. Where I finally let it down enough to get them.

The Cost
of Pretending

"Because the sunset, like survival, exists only on the verge
of its own disappearing. To be gorgeous, you must first
be seen, but to be seen allows you to be hunted."

—OCEAN VUONG,

***ON EARTH, WE'RE BRIEFLY GORGEOUS* (2019)**

I was in the fifth grade when my father started pumping the rules of "pretend" into my veins. We had just seen *Peter Pan*. It wasn't my first Broadway show (that was *Beauty and the Beast*), but this one, *Pan*, left a big impact on your boy. I was smitten. I didn't want to be a singing teacup, I wanted to be a flying child who never grew up (some people out there have an ongoing debate as to whether I have achieved this), I walked out of the theater, arms in a T—acting like I was flying through the streets of NYC, pleading to the gods, announcing to anyone who would listen, especially my father, "That's what I want, I want to fly around like I'm Peter!"

To which my pops responded: "Never gonna happen, *mijo*, Peter's played by a woman. You are not that."

Before I could wallow in my defeat, he said, "Hey don't cry, get it together." It was still light out, so he took me to Central

Park. He got us two hot dogs and introduced me to his favorite game, one I still play to this day, called "Where they going? Where they coming from? Why do they walk that way?"

My pops was convinced that if you watch anything long enough, you can become an expert at it. You get to know how it lives, how it breathes. He'd say: "You want to be rich, hang out with rich people; you want to be smart, hang out with smart people; you want to be funny, hang out with funny people. Whatever you want to be, put yourself there till it comes true. You gotta play the part *mijo*, play the part. You take the life you want, and you make the life you want."

"Play the part," and just like that, it all made sense. My pops was the king at playing the part.

My pops was the superintendent of a 164-unit building in Queens. He knew everyone and everyone knew him, or at least a version of him. He had as many masks as keys, and he had a lot of keys. I watched him chat, mimic, and play with everybody. One key at a time: the Russians, the Dominicans, the Puerto Ricans, the Jews, his white bosses, his Black brothers and friends, the hood rats, the street rats, the young kids, the old kids, the senile, the clientele, the doctors.

"*Mijo*, you take the life you want, and you make the life you want."

I noticed early on how many different people my father could become. Sometimes it was a handshake, sometimes it was a head nod, sometimes his voice went really low, and sometimes it went high. Often it was him laughing at really bad jokes nobody should ever laugh at, sometimes it was a wider smile then I ever saw or got. He spoke Russian—"*Dos vidaniya, Kak dela?*" He

spoke street—"Yo, get off my property!" He spoke Spanish—
"*Oye, Flaco, cómo estás?*" And of course white—"Yes, sir, yes,
ma'am."

I thought my pops was the coolest and flyest person I
knew. I was just under five feet and about to enter the tenth
grade. I was not the coolest or flyest. I was not my father or
the kids at the park or anyone I wished I could be. But I still
didn't really understand why my cool as hell, Dominican
Samuel L. Jackson (the *Pulp Fiction* one), mad-wisdom,
roller-skating, DJing Central Park parties, king of cool pops
needed to be anything other than who he was. Why he needed
to pretend, shapeshift, and fit into so many different boxes. I
would call him out on it: "Pops, why you gotta act so different
with everybody?"

"Hey, that's not true, mind your business, leave me alone,"
he'd say.

But it was true. He did act different with everybody. So why
fight to not just accept it? Maybe, it was habitual, a second,
third, and fourth skin that he didn't even know about.

Maybe his IV full of *pretend* and *fake it till you make it* was so
deeply attached to him, he forgot it was there, his many masks
and personas becoming one with his blood. That game in the
park was just one of many games and lessons designed to teach
me how to pretend, how to fit in.

While shining his shoes, my pops would utter proclamations
like "It's all about how you enter a room, *mijo*, because people
are always gonna be watching you. Always. So, enter with your
head high and shoes that shine. If you can't afford much, get a
great pair of shoes and some shoehorns, always shoehorns."

When I told my pops I wanted to play pretend for a living, that I wanted to be an actor, that I wanted to go to Hollywood, he said: "It's gonna be tough, but look the part. Pretend. Fake it till you make it."

Right, but I didn't look the part, I didn't look like Pacey Witter from *Dawson's Creek*. When he got frosted tips in season 2, I wanted them so badly. I begged my mom, but she wisely said, "No."

It didn't matter that I didn't look the part, I was going to make my pops proud. I wanted to show him I could play the game of pretend as well as him, I could build a life of fitting in and being like "them." By any means necessary. I could be the Dominican Peter Pan, *Pedrito Panito*.

To accomplish this, I did exactly what my pops said—in the park, any park, in the streets, I sat, and I watched. Perfecting my masks and becoming what I wanted, no matter what.

The great lecture hall where it all went down was the NYC subway. For years, during high school, my hour-long subway rides were my symposium. The tunnels and cramped cars were a master class on how to be something else. The focus I absolutely failed to bring into my schooling and classrooms was only because I was saving it for my real studies: watching people who seemed to have it all figured out. I would sit back on the train and watch their *carry yourself with the confidence of a mediocre white man* confidence. I now know this as privilege, but back then I just knew it as a key to opening doors, a key I, too, could have.

I became this master chameleon, composing myself out of pieces of everyone else. I knew I had the power to make myself and remake myself over and over again. I walked the NYC subways like I was about to be asked for a dissertation on what every Upper East Side and Wall Street yuppie who seemed to have cash and clout did, wore, and smelt like. I sat across from these chosen ones on the train, I mimicked their postures, I blinked when they blinked, I became a mirror. I was in tune with the rise and fall of each one of their exhales and exclamations, mimicking their ability to maneuver the world. I watched how the boys held the girls. I watched how the girls held the boys. When they whispered a joke in an ear that caused a laugh, I would whisper and laugh. If some dude was successfully mackin' it to some guy or some girl, I could just take the essence of that. Make it my own. If someone laughed in a cool way, I could take the essence of that. The way they licked their lips, the way they held their bag, how they walked into a room, how they left. Walk like this, and smile like that.

At night I would sit in my room and replay these scenes over and over (remember I'm a theater school kid). I was crafting a playbook. Plays and scenes that I would whip out in different scenarios, I would practice them so that when the moment arrived, and I had the shot to impress someone, to come off as more than what I actually was, I could put on a character—a mask—and execute it to perfection.

I was an everything-man and a nothing all at the same time. If I think about it, I am astounded at the speed with which I constantly adapted myself to new surroundings. Everybody knew me, but nobody knew me. I went to school in the Upper East Side and was chilling. I hung out with my best friend in the Bronx and was chillin'. I lived among wealthy Jews and went to a Jewish afterschool program, I went to at least thirty-seven bar mitzvahs by the time I was thirteen, so many my mom had to start regifting stuff from around the house, so many that when I turned thirteen, the community and the Jewish afterschool program at the Queens Central Y decided, "Chris needs one of these, too."

So, they threw me my very own bar mitzvah in Flushing Meadow Park (home of the 1964 World's Fair). There was grape juice, Manischewitz, challah bread, "Baruch atah Adoshem"— the whole nine yards. How many Dominicans from Queens do you know who have had a bar mitzvah?

The party, the backyard, the hood, the school, the social setting became my battlefield, and language became my weapon. My tongue can elegantly wear many a disguise and mask. But, the one thing my tongue can't do or pretend its way through (trust me, I've tried) is speaking Spanish. Yep.

There's the rub, eh?

It's an embarrassing fact that I have kept to myself for a very long time. Until a couple months ago when I started taking weekly Spanish lessons, and they have emotionally been kicking my ass. After class one day I called my Puerto Rican buddy who is in the same boat, in fact he introduced me to our Spanish teacher. He wanted to chat with his grandmother before she passed. For one of my grandmothers, I didn't have that chance. For the other, I hope I get to.

"Eli, it sucks learning a language you feel like you should already know," I told him. "It sucks."

Our Spanish classes are taught by an organization that focuses on working with folks who identify as Latino or Hispanic but don't speak the language. A lot of traumas come up in these classes, a lot of the sessions are really just about moving on past the embarrassment and shame.

One woman from Honduras was sharing with us why she decided to study Spanish in the first place: "In my family making ourselves closer to whiteness was always the goal. Which meant speaking Spanish was not a priority. My whiteness was celebrated a lot in my family. I was much lighter than all my sisters, and they constantly told me it would take me far in this country."

This really struck a chord with me. I asked Eli: "You think our parents not teaching us Spanish was an 'I want to be white thing' or an 'I don't wanna be Brown thing'? Both our older siblings speak Spanish, but not us. You never think about why?"

"All the time."

"Okay, so, why?" I insisted. "Why did my sister get to visit the DR every summer as a child, and I didn't?" I pressed on, "Do you think it's because they were like, I want my son to be white or because I don't want my son to be anything but white?"

"It's two sides of the same coin," he answered.

Meaning whatever the answer is, it's not pretty. If it's framed as approaching whiteness, it is also the pushing away of something: color, culture, identity. Because wrapped up and embedded in this made-up concept of whiteness and its worth are so many cultures, colors, and identities. There is no supremacy, only supreme appropriation. And yet, in our assimilation, we have failed to see that our cultures weren't lost. They were stolen.

To praise the motherland is not a clear disowning of the new land. Vice versa, to praise the new land doesn't have to be a full disowning of the mother. To want your child to be a living, breathing example of where their ancestors come from versus focusing on what's here, what's present, not what was. I can't call my parents out on their shit because then I'd have to call myself on my own shit—like why it never mattered to me until now to actually take the steps to learn Spanish. There are a lot of complexities that go into raising a child and just keeping that child alive, then mix in not just trying to keep them alive, but giving said child possibilities, then add a dash of what is lost in the search for upward mobility, and all these complexities go way beyond the number of languages that child speaks.

We had no final answers that afternoon, just more feelings and some more studying to do. We drank our beers and went home.

A couple of weeks later in my email I received a poem from the Poetry Foundation (I get a poem a week from them), it was called "Richard Cory," it was by Edwin Arlington Robinson and written in 1897 . . .

> Whenever Richard Cory went down town,
> We people on the pavement looked at him:
> He was a gentleman from sole to crown,
> Clean favored, and imperially slim
>
> . . .
> And he was rich—yes, richer than a king—
> And admirably schooled in every grace:
> In fine, we thought that he was everything
> To make us wish that we were in his place.

This poem is the story of a man who seems to have it all. The people of the town place Richard Cory on a pedestal. They look up to him and want to be just like him. Everyone has a Richard Cory in their life, whether it's a person or a job, a partner, a dream; everyone has an ideal something in their minds that make us wish we were in their place/that place/their shoes.

I read this poem, and it clicked.

I immediately texted it to Eli and said, "This, this is why us speaking Spanish wasn't high on the list."

Imagine Richard Cory is the American ideal life. The ideal American human. Imagine showing up as an immigrant in this country, an outsider of any kind, and how envious you are of Richard Cory and the way he effortlessly moves through the world. Like he floats and you walk, shit, most of the time you're actually running. He takes naps, and you can't get enough sleep. He saves money, and all you seem to be able to do is not have enough.

For the most part, all immigrants, all BIPOC, all melanin and culture rich, the entirety of the global majority in the United States know that if they want to become successful, real, authentically American Richard Corys, they must in some way reduce their fealty to their native country and native skin and regard it as secondary, subordinate, in order to emphasize their whiteness. They know it even if they don't know it.

Sometimes we assimilate in conscious ways and sometimes in unconscious ways. There are people who absolutely refuse to assimilate, or evade assimilation due to environment. Lack of proximity to whiteness eradicates the need or urgency to align with it. An Asian-American child in an Asian community, a young Black adult in D.C. or Oakland, a Latina in Miami, etc. These Black and Brown folks may not assimilate because there was neither reason or appeal.

I must acknowledge my privilege of growing up in New York City. That city taught me more about moving through the world than any book. New York is special in that you can see how people of color adapt, adjust, shift, and maintain.

Assimilation is deeply nuanced regarding the intersection of race and identity. While there is loss that comes with reducing one's identity to assimilate, there are also cultural and societal gains. I am seeking those gains. Assimilation isn't a "you do it or don't do it" type of thing. At times it just buries and hides itself under your skin. Many people will assimilate in certain ways but remain uncompromising in others. There's the "yes sir, yes ma'am" bill collector voice used in predominantly white spaces. Temporary moments where the mask comes off or on, and we must think, vote, speak, and live in ways that adhere to white supremacist and patriarchal standards. Almost everybody has done this in one way or another. Suppress their true identity. But there are consequences of existing in assimilation for too long.

Assimilation is as nuanced as love, it doesn't look the same on everyone, it doesn't express itself in the same ways. Sometimes it leaves trauma, and sometimes it doesn't. Sometimes it's violent, and sometimes it's peaceful. You can be obsessed with it, and you could be kind of chill about it. It can keep you up at night, and it can even feel kind of good. It has existed since the sapiens decided to come together and wipe out the Neanderthals. Since the sapiens decided to create power structures, government, policy, and laws. Since the birth of capitalism, since the birth of one person selling you something you were told you needed.

Assimilation is in our blood, right next to survival, it is inherited and handed down from ancestor to ancestor. Assimilate or die is what is sold to us in subtle and unsubtle ways. The Spanish consumed the Indigenous and raped, shamed, and murdered whoever wouldn't join them. The Catholic Church swallowed pagan signifiers as a way of maintaining power. The British consumed a whole bunch of cultures that wouldn't act right. Cultural appropriators feast on the cultures of marginalized groups without affording them any reward, recognition, or power. America has been trying to consume color and culture for as far back as the birthing of America.

I read this poem, and I knew that my parents moved themselves and their family closer to the ways and mannerisms of the white people who were signing their checks, and those checks allowed us to eat, to live, to maintain.

Last year, I was having lunch with my parents when I read them this poem. I told them: "I've been taking Spanish classes y'all, and it's really hard. It brings up a lot of insecurities." Then, I asked them: "Why was it never a big deal that I spoke Spanish? Why was I never sent to the DR to spend summers with Abuelita like Lauren [my sister] was?"

"I'm sorry, we didn't push for it," my mom said.

"I was never able to have a real conversation with *mamita* [my mother's mother] before she died. I never got to hear about her childhood in Colombia, her stories, her recipes, her wisdom. Friends tell me about how funny or cool their grandparents were, and I keep quiet, because I didn't have the luxury of knowing her like that. I hate that."

"I'm not gonna apologize to you, Chris," my dad said. "Look at your life. Your life is good, yes?"

"Yes, my life is good."

"And now you want to know more about your history, and you want to speak the language, great. *Estoy aquí. Hablemos juntos en Español. Bien. Perfecto*—but don't make a big deal of it. Look what you've accomplished, Spanish or no Spanish, look at your life. We did the best we could, and we think it was pretty damn good."

After a couple minutes of silence, they both began telling me about watching their Brown parents bust their asses only to continue busting their asses. How it never ended, and what did they have to show for it? Nothing. Both their parents didn't speak English, and what did they have to show for it? Nothing. Both had parents who worked tirelessly till their bodies physically couldn't do it anymore.

"We didn't want you and your sister to experience the shit that we experienced. We wanted you to have more. Be more."

They wanted us to be Richard Corys. They didn't want us to hustle and hustle only to hustle some more.

They did it for us. They each worked two jobs—a 9 a.m. to 5 p.m. and a 7 p.m. to 3 a.m. During the day my pops was the super at our apartment building up in Queens, and at night he was a doorman at another building. My mom worked at an OB/GYN office by day and ran the desk at an emergency room by night. Sometimes I wouldn't even see them for a whole week. Which is wild because my pops worked in the building where we lived.

My sister and I, we raised each other over that year. Well, she raised me, to be honest. She cooked most meals, and I chipped in here and there. My sister and I were cooking and doing our own laundry from the moment we were tall enough to reach the necessary buttons and knobs. During that time our small apartment in Queens seemed like a mansion without my parents' love.

And then one day, after barely seeing them for a year, they called my sister and I on the phone to say, "Yo, we bought a place, and we're picking you up, and we're headed to Six Flags, and we got fast passes!"

My parents later told me, "You two were more excited about the fast passes than the house."

Makes sense, we didn't yet understand the significance of owning something, having equity, and giving their kids a shot at the American Dream, but no waiting in lines—this we understood!

My parents stayed committed to playing the game. For us, for their kids, for our future, and for the American Dream. As my mom explained, they decided that in order for me and my sister to thrive in this country, "we had to live above our means, we were the richest no rich family." Because in order to be Richard Corys, we needed to be as American as we could be, and my parents needed to set that example for us from the jump by any means necessary. Even when family and friends accused them of abandoning their roots, like when I was thirteen years old and out of nowhere in the middle of a big merengue salsa-Dominican-bachata-me-and-all-my-cousins-shindig-party in Queens, my father's cousin called my pops "fake." Fake. A shouting match began, and then one cousin yelled, "Look who it is, the Blancitos!" Followed up with, "When are you gonna stop trying to be white?"

"White," which is really just a comment on power. Like who isn't trying to have power?

My parents shrugged it off, because those opinions didn't matter, or in my pops's own words: "Fuck 'em. You make your own life. They're just jealous."

My folks played the game and never once called out the system, because, if you say "Fuck you" to the powers that be, fuck you to pretending, fuck you to assimilation, fuck you to the system, then the system says it right back, and then you might lose your "freedom," you might lose whatever "mobility" you think you have.

I used to be angry at my parents, wondering why they seemed to let go of their past. I thought that they believed that in order to get ahead, something must be left behind. I thought they weren't proud of where they came from.

Now, I know better. I am no longer mad. I think my parents did what so many Brown Americans are forced to do, assimilate and pretend in hopes of possibility for their kids, so they don't have to watch them go hungry. Assimilation or pretending, or whatever you wanna call it, it's not a thing to condemn, the need to assimilate into another culture to avoid discrimination and achieve advancement is pretty universal for any outsider. It's a part of the overarching, vaguely defined American, Black, Brown, and Indigenous experience. Now, I thank them. Because for better or worse, I learned how to navigate this America in a body of color. It is a necessary and valuable skill, and I have learned well.

But where they did it just to get by, I do it in the hope of getting ahead.

I'm not less, and my parents didn't let go of anything on purpose or because they were done with their Latinidad, because that's not true. I still went to a Colombian bakery every Saturday, followed by Don Francisco and *Sábado Gigante* that same night. We had the best Chino-Dominicano food in Queens at least twice a month, I'm talking a bowl of wonton soup next to some killer *maduro* and *mangu*. My parents were simply building a life as best as they knew how. A good life. No, my home wasn't especially filled with flags of my parent's respective homelands, but it didn't have *any* flags for that matter. It wasn't decked out in Santeria Orishas, Oshun, or rosary beads, there weren't maracas lying around, it was just a home. We ate rice and beans, but we also ate a lot of frozen tortellini, and a lot of pastrami on rye from the corner diner that knew all our names and never handed us a menu, because we knew it by heart—walking into a place and being known is something my father takes significant pride in.

My parents did salsa dance a lot, and that was fucking glorious. My father floated and my mother levitated, they both shined. Watching my parents dance was like being taken to another time and another place, *Dirty Dancing: Havana Nights*, except starring two Brown People. Watching them do their thing was mesmerizing. They also danced the hustle, a lot. They danced all the dances. They are kids of the disco era. They always had on music, and they were always dancing.

I learned a lot more from them than just another language or how to pretend and fit in, I learned about love and sacrifice, I learned rhythm, I learned how to properly scratch a record Grand Master Flash style, how to cook, how to be self-sufficient, how to dance, how to hustle, and how to care.

I learned how to be a New Yorker—I hold this in high regard—because the city I grew up in is a big deal to me. My parents taught me that being a New Yorker means something a world apart from being Brown, Dominican, Colombian, Afro-Latino, Afro-Taino, Caribbean, or American, we were New Yorkers.

All that said, it is the very last paragraph in the Richard Cory poem that mattered most to my mother and father, my homie, and just about anyone:

We thought that he was everything
To make us wish that we were in his place.

So on we worked, and waited for the light,
And went without the meat, and cursed the bread;
And Richard Cory, one calm summer night,
Went home and put a bullet through his head.

Imagine, you work your whole life to become Richard Cory, you pretend and pretend, but Richard Cory is actually miserable, he's not the ideal you thought he was. You get to the place you always wanted to be, and you realize that it is nothing like what you thought it was.

I wonder if this awareness of my own pretending to fit in happened too late for me—like a burn that keeps on burning from the inside. Because once you burn yourself, it's already too late, the damage is already done. It took too long for your brain to warn you, to tell you to stop. And now that you're singed, the skin is actually still burning itself, that's why they say run it under cool water for twenty minutes (but who has twenty minutes?) because the skin holds the heat, the body holds the trauma.

If skin can hold heat for twenty minutes, imagine how long it can hold the need to become something else.

There is an actual medical term for all this, for a person who tries and tries and tries to accomplish something, in order to be seen, in order to be enough, in order to not be forgotten: it's called John Henryism.

The term was conceived in the 1970s by African American epidemiologist and public health researcher Sherman James.

He was investigating racial health disparities between Blacks and others in North Carolina. One of the people he interviewed was a Black man named John Henry Martin. John Henry Martin worked hard with only a second-grade education and freed himself and his children from the sharecropper system, he accumulated seventy-five acres of his own farmland by his forties, but by his fifties, he had hypertension, arthritis, and severe peptic ulcer disease.

According to Sherman James, John Henry Martin and his circumstances were evocative of the "steel driving man," a popular folk hero and subject of many a blues song. That John Henry was an African American man who was in a race against a steam-powered machine drilling holes for a railroad tunnel, a race that he won only to die in victory with the hammer still in hand as his heart gave out from stress. The John Henry story also served as proof that the industrial revolution could not beat human labor. In many ways, it defended the South's pro-slavery position. Enslaved people are more valuable than machines and were therefore a necessary component of a robust, successful economy.

Sherman James tells us that the physiological costs of competing for praise from another person is high. I have no doubt, because I carry it daily, a steady anxiety that I feel in my gut and in my heart every day. Hence all the reaching, grasping, and changing of myself, purchasing and practicing new things, new experiments, so that I can be more worthy of being loved. But it's also a false kind of love we get when we pretend, because what we truly want is to be loved for who we are.

Knowing this I can positively switch that habit into something else. There is an extraordinary power in the rejection of someone else's story, in taking someone who has been devalued and devoured by white supremacy and holding them in high esteem. Transforming all this internalized supremacy into the confidence to be myself, from the inside out.

The Richard Cory and John Henry curses can begin to break with me. I will no longer let the "ideal image" sold to me on a daily basis run my life. My value is already here. I don't have to pretend. I don't have to fake it. My Latinidad card is in my hands no matter how good my Spanish is, I'm holding it. The words I use to describe it may change (depending on how frequently I show up to Spanish class), and my understanding of it may shift, but it is mine. I will begin to own my Brownness. For everything it is and isn't. Own my experience and share that experience. So that those who come after *me* can begin to do the same. No shame in what we are. No shame in what we are not. I don't have to be more than this.

Always Lie
When Someone
Asks If You Meditate

"Why do you sit? Even chickens sit. Why do you sit?"

—YONGHWA LEE,

MY TEACHER AT THE DIAMOND ZEN CENTER

She was always cool, super cool. Everything about her was cool. One of those people who make life look effortless. Who make the simplest things like taking out the trash seem magical? A person who doesn't care what you think, and so you care what she thinks. I wanted to have that type of touch and magic. I wanted her to think I was cool. At that point in my life, I wanted anyone to think I was cool. Who am I kidding? I recently bought an Instagram ad. This means I actually paid Instagram money so that I could be seen as cool (insert "mind explosion" emoji).

So, Sophia, this incredibly down to earth and vibey half-Black, half-Asian woman from New York comes up to me and asks, "Do you meditate?"

Without a glitch, I confidently said: "Yeah, of course, of course I meditate. For sure, I meditate all the time."

"I meditate all the time," who says that? At that point in my life I had never meditated. In my experience, Latin kids from Queens did not meditate. I was a sophomore in college and meditating was low on my hierarchy of needs. Between beer pong, Shakespeare (again, I was in theater school), drugs, staying up till 6:00 a.m., and doing it all over again, there wasn't much inclination or motivation for other activities.

But I liked this woman a lot. I had for a while, and I knew she was tapped into something that I had no idea about, and I would have said yes to whatever she asked me—you like looking stupid? "Yes, ma'am, absolutely, I love looking stupid."

I could have stopped with the very suave "I meditate all the time" line. Though, and I'm not sure why I said this, I don't know if it was about making the lie seem more believable or because I thought it would further the conversation, I also decided to throw in a solid "I do it twice a day, how about you?"

I liked her a lot, and for some reason, she liked me. She definitely liked that I "meditated," so we started dating.

She would spend the night, then wake up early to "sit" (aka meditate), and ask if I wanted to join, and I'd always have some excuse not to join her, "Oh, I'll do it tonight," or, "After class." I tried, I did. I hit up the library and got every book I could, on Zen, on meditating, meditating for dummies, I started googling, and it just never stuck.

For starters, it was hard. Just sitting in stillness can be boring. I didn't understand it. I didn't understand why a person just sits. It didn't feel like what the books told me, it felt like I was doing it wrong, and so why do it in the first place?

Our relationship wasn't all lies. It was actually pretty great. Two New Yorkers trapped in a very white suburb studying theater. For hours, we would just smoke weed and talk about art. We had a really good time. We'd been dating for a year strong when on my twenty-first birthday, she took me out to this great fancy dinner. At dinner she was so giddy, she had this huge smile, excited to give me the gift she got for me. I thought dinner was the gift, but I wasn't gonna say no to that new pair of Chuck Taylors I mentioned wanting.

Then she handed me a skinny envelope . . . Is my girlfriend giving me cash, like a bar mitzvah?

I open the envelope, and inside are two plane tickets to Massachusetts. "What's in Massachusetts?" I ask.

"A weeklong Vipassana silent retreat," she says.

(Oh shit.)

She says: "I can tell how hard you've been working, and I really think this will take your practice to the next level. I want you to have this."

(Oh shit.)

I have to tell her, I have to confess, I have to tell her Allen Iverson style: "Practice, what practice? We talking about practice?" I have to tell her that there is no practice, that I wasn't built for meditating. I like to write everything down. I like to talk. I have extremely tight hips. I can't go there, I can't be quiet for seven days, because I can't be quiet for thirty seconds. I can't. I tried, I did. I went to the library and read the books, I promise you, I tried. Just tell her Chris: "I lied to you. I'm sorry. You are so cool, and this is so great, and I just wanted it to work, but I can't turn twenty-one in silence, I can't do that, no one should do that."

But I don't say any of that. I say: "Wow. Wow. Thank you. I'm so excited. Wow."

She starts to cry, and all I can think is, what is wrong with me? She's so happy for me and for us—because she's joining. She's so happy that she could give me this, that we will get to share it.

For those of you who don't know what a silent retreat is, it's basically just that. A time to remain silent. In this case, it was seven days of Vipassana meditation, no phone, no books, no journal, no talking, no nothing but silence and observing your own thoughts.

It's my girlfriend's third silent retreat at IMS, the Insight Meditation Society in Barry, Massachusetts, *her third*. As she has explained it to me, "A silent retreat is more than just being silent, Chris, the retreat gives us an opportunity to look inward and process our thoughts in a calm, constructive way." This is a lie, but we will get back to this.

The whole flight there, I wanted to tell her. I don't. We get there, we check in, we meet some people in the moments before the talking stops, and I'm quickly assigned the job of washing dishes. Everyone is assigned a task of some sort to help break up the monotony of nothingness. Little do they know, I *love* washing dishes so this might not be so bad.

She and I are the only people of color on the retreat. Normally, I would complain about this to the higher-ups, but technically I can't talk. At first, it really isn't so bad, it's kind of nice actually. Sit for thirty min, walk for thirty min. Sit for thirty min, walk for thirty min. Sit for thirty min, walk for thirty min. Easy.

Easy for one round. Then it quickly evolves to miserable. Quickly everything goes sour. This is not like the magazines where toned white women with lean arms in prayer position are smiling ear to ear. It's more like being trapped in a phone booth with a lunatic. All day. Except I am the lunatic who is now reminding me how I don't belong. How I lied, how I took advantage of this person's trust, how I always take advantage and push my luck, how I don't really care about a practice being sacred to a person, how I don't really listen, how I'll never make it, how I'm not enough, how I don't belong in this space, how I don't have the strength or the skill or the talent or the worth . . . and it goes on and on like this. On and on and on.

When you aren't speaking, an hour is an eternity. When you aren't doing anything but sitting in silence for thirty minutes and then walking in silence for thirty minutes, an hour is excruciating. Any human being who thinks there isn't enough time in the day, stop checking your phone and sending emails and watching Netflix, and just sit. Then tell me there isn't enough time in the day. Time is long, short, or as vicious and never ending as you need it to be. Einstein wasn't wrong, time is absolutely relative, a minute sitting on a hot stove versus a minute next to the person you love—relative.

Six hours in, and I hit a wall (yes, we are still on day one): Chris, quit and tell her the truth or figure it out.

I choose to figure it out. Why? Motivational reasons like, I'm not a quitter, and everything happens for a reason. But also practical ones like my flight back to LA isn't for another week, and there is no way I can afford to change it. When not speaking, in a matter of seconds, you figure out a lot of things. One second, you know everything, you are tapped in, tuned in, turned on, the next second, you know nothing.

On day two (just day two!), I become obsessed with Michael Jackson's "Rock with You." I start analyzing it word by word, like it's some great philosophical essay. I realize that what he's saying is he wants to be intimate with this person, not just sex, but like true close intimacy *all night* until the sun comes up—he doesn't care about being tired the next day—he is present and in the now—and what matters more than presence?

It was day two when one woman woke up in the middle of the night, stole all the Post-it notes she could find and wrote on them, "Don't step here," placing them on every inch of wood floor that creaked. One of the retreat facilitators told us this happens because your mind does not like being watched, so it makes up these epic stories and missions so as to take back control and not be witnessed. Her mind said don't look at me, look at everything squeaking around you, focus on that for a while.

It was around this time that I was convinced my girlfriend was mad at me, that she knew I lied, and she was furious. Mainly because she wouldn't look at me, even though the rules of the retreat are to *not* make direct eye contact, so as not to take people out of their experience. My rational mind understood that she was following the rules, but my get-obsessed-place-Post-it-notes-everywhere mind, the mind that doesn't like being watched, my guilt-ridden mind, my tiny ego mind, did not understand this at all.

She was definitely mad at me.

I wrote her a letter asking her if she was okay, telling her I missed her, fun thoughts I'd had, and I passed it to her in the hallway like I was passing off a shank. Much to my relief and surprise she broke the rules and wrote one back. It became a thing. This happened for about one to two very long days. At this point, we are communicating, and we are not following the rules.

This entire note-passing thing was the most entertaining part of my day. It really stole the focus. All this note passing eventually leads us to her dorm room, together and silent, engaging in what can only be described as very quiet sex. And now the thing I feared in the initial letter about her being mad at me has actually come true. Now she's actually mad at me. She feels horrible because I distracted her, I took her out of her place; I made it about the outside versus the inside. I brought her down with me.

It's day three and a half, and I am not feeling happier. This isn't what the articles, Eckhart Tolle, or the self-help books promised. It isn't working. I can't do it. I have to come up with a reason to like being here or I will lose my mind. I tell myself, "I like meditating because it makes me a better artist."

At this point in my life, being an artist is the one thing that makes it all make sense for me, the glue with which I use to keep myself together. I say: "Meditating is an art lesson. Be present, be in the moment, and listen. It's all for the art." This reasoning carries me for a few days.

Day five, a woman yells from the back of the meditation hall. She yells like she just lost everything she loves. She yells a yell that even now (the thought of it) brings tears to my eyes. She yells a blood-curdling yell. She has to be dragged out. Dragged and yelling the whole time. The facilitator says very peacefully, "It happens, it happens, may we continue to practice and send love."

It happens, huh?

All the questions in my mind, they just keep on coming. The doubts are endless. The revelations about who I am, what I am, and why I waste so much time concerned with frivolous but also important and completely tiny things are exhausting and daunting, and I still think she hates me. I still haven't told her the truth, and I'm not sure if I ever will.

I make it to the end of seven days, and I'm not sure if I'm a better person or not. I'm not really sure what happened, and yet

I feel changed. Internally, like I traveled. That's how they talk about it in the Tibetan Book of the Dead. Tibetans are psychonauts—less concerned with exploring outer space and much more interested in the depth of inner space. At the end of this retreat I had found a little more inner space, like something new had dug its way in and something old had dug its way out.

One evening during a Dharma Talk (think TedTalk with a Buddhist twist) there was this quote that was shared, and it has stuck with me ever since:

> I knew early on that finding truth is not the same as find-ing happiness. You aspire to see the truth, but once you have seen it, you cannot avoid suffering. Otherwise, you've seen nothing at all.

Or as I've said before, ignorance is bliss *until* you've tasted bliss. Then the rest is just ignorance.

When the retreat was over, so was our relationship, not im-mediately, but soon enough after. I told her the truth. I couldn't walk back without moving forward, and I couldn't move for-ward walking backward. When words returned, we had none left for each other. On the day we decided to go our separate ways, I told her, and still tell her to this day: "Thank you for the greatest gift I ever received. Meditation changed my life, and I likely never would have found my way to it in such an intense way without you. Thank you for changing my life."

Since I left that first retreat thirteen years ago, for the most part, I have meditated every morning since. Nothing crazy, what started as five-minute daily sits now lives in the thirty- to forty-minute range. Sometimes I meditate on my own death, sometimes I try to just breathe and smile (as Thich Nhat Hanh advises), sometimes I can't stop thinking and stop before the timer is up, sometimes I fall asleep during the sit. I have had Post-it note moments. I have had scream it out moments. I have had beautiful sits and torturous ones. I have gone deeper into my practice by studying with different teachers, different teachings, in different communities, and yet I continually feel like the outlier in this practice.

I feel like I don't fit in, racially and/or socioeconomically. The value of what I've learned has been stripped and bleached by consumerism and the wellness community.

All around me are magazines and billboards trying to sell me happiness, as if self-care helps someone without health insurance. Ads filled with affluent-looking white people with slender arms overhead or hands in prayer position with their eyes closed and meditating. I have an Instagram feed that is covered in almond milk lattes and kombuchas with beautiful people who look nothing like me in a stunning garden backdrop, holding acai bowls, chanting, a ton of vegan food, essential oils and on their way to a Kundalini-mindful-juice-colonic-sound-bath in Bali or Costa Rica, "exotic" retreats in places where many of the locals live in poverty, but where the economy revolves around catering to white Westerners who come for a luxury spiritual experience, ignoring what their systems of abuse and oppression have done to the same people.

Where are the people who look like me?

My Saturday morning yoga class is made up of twelve white women and me. My Tuesday evening sitting session, same thing, not another person of color. There is not another person of color in many of the yoga classes I attend. There is not another person of color in my Sunday morning meditation at the Kadampa Center. There is not another person of color in this Y7 class, a heated, candlelit hip-hop yoga class that is taking over New York and Los Angeles, a place where the walls read, "A Tribe Called Sweat," and Drake blasts over the speaker. And I'm not saying that there aren't any Black and Brown-led wellness spaces. I am sure there are, but they are few and far between in my pocket of Los Angeles.

What intention are we setting? What messages are we sending with the images portrayed by this very specific-looking health and happiness community? A whole industry of coaching, websites, books, e-books, audio books, seminars, workshops, documentaries, $20 coffees full of fat, that sells me a thousand different ways to help me change, because I guess I need to change, at a price point that is well, quite frankly, not easily accessible.

A whole industry telling me that where I am and what I am is not enough. For the record, meditation (as I see it) is not about becoming a better version of yourself, it's not about being more productive.

Amazon just recently started inviting employees who often live off food stamps and make just enough to clear the federal poverty line a way to calm their minds while their bodies are worked to the bone. Amazon installed meditation kiosks in its warehouses. It's a despair closet, where employees can watch videos of guided meditations, they call it "AmaZen." This is the same company that is often criticized for not allowing their employees enough time to actually pee. During one heatwave in Pennsylvania, rather than bringing in AC units, Amazon chose the more cost-efficient solution of parking ambulances outside the doors to collect the people who collapsed. Alex Press, a Gizmodo staff writer wrote, "A Porta Potty would be more useful."

Meditation cannot occur at the expense of human rights. Meditation (as I see it) is about noticing the flaws, noticing the suffering, and being present to it. In fact, meditation has a long history and connection to social justice and human rights, even though the Dalai Lama has currently been reduced to a Western fantasy of serenity. Remember, monks once lit themselves on fire in order to make a stand for justice and peace, and Cesar Chavez used meditation during his hunger strikes.

A very good friend of mine is a yoga teacher, she is white, and one day she was teaching while wearing a T-shirt that had Ganesh on it, Ganesh Chaturthi to be exact, the very revered and highly worshipped Hindu god. He has an elephant head and many arms. Ganesh is the remover of obstacles, the patron of arts and sciences, and the god of intellect and wisdom, among other things. I'm sure you've seen him.

After class, an Indian woman went up to my friend and said, "I think it's offensive that you are wearing that and appropriating my culture." This really fucked with my homegirl. She would never want to do something like that consciously, but also, she got the shirt at Urban Outfitters.

How do I feel about the fact that these technologies, teachings, and practices that come from the nonwhite world are now predominately white facing and brought to us by white bodies? I am glad the teachings are here for me to access. Truly, I am. Daily silence for me is not about being better but just being. For a couple moments I'm not running or distracting myself, I'm not trying to fix anything, and if I am, then I just sit with it and get intimate with that desire. If only for a second I am able to leave myself alone. In those moments, the noise is quieted, and it's worth it.

I also acknowledge that many of the successful teachers, schools, and books that gained popularity and brought these teachings from the East to the West in the '70s and '80s were created and written by white people: Tara Brach, Jack Kornfield, Ram Dass, Jon Kabat-Zinn, Bernie Glassman, Sharon Salzberg. I have read a book and listened to a talk by each and every one of these wonderful teachers, and I would recommend them to others who are interested. But these bodies being the pillars (then and now) of these teachings traveling west is dangerous, it assumes that the world doesn't contain multiple identities. And yet, I wonder who is next? What does inclusivity and diversity look like in a world of spiritual technologies, self-help, and eastern teachings becoming westernized? Can white wellness people carefully consider why their offerings might not appeal to BIPOC for reasons that go beyond personal preference?

Because spirituality cranked through the engine of capitalism, it has nothing to do with spirituality. It's dilution in the name of selling, which is also an aspect of cultural appropriation, because despite what all the articles and self-help books tell you, meditation and mindfulness is not just a way to be more productive, and he/she who wears the most Lululemon is not the happiest or most enlightened being in the room (also, an average pair of Lululemon pants will set you back $118).

I'm not mad. Really, I'm not. I like yoga, I like meditating, I like kombucha, I dig it all. I'm your client. I'm not telling you to stop drinking green juice. Drink your ten-dollar green juice knowing there are also places without clean water and operating sewer systems. And buy your ten-dollar green juice from people of color. I'm saying that it isn't fair to put a price tag on everything, and that *all* humans deserve to be in the running for a more peaceful mind and broader life perspective. That's what meditation has done for me, it has not made me the happiest person alive, but it has allowed me the perspective to meet myself over and over again, among all that will be smashed so I can remember that we are all in need of love and hope, that we are all doing our best, and that each moment will eventually pass. I have not mastered it, far from it, and yet it has given me a great gift, one that I think should be accessible to everyone.

I am beyond grateful that I, a Dominican and Colombian kid from Queens, came to value this education, this time spent meeting myself and envisioning a better world and a better self. I am in awe and often brought to tears that a lie and a single encounter with another person of color showed me that it was okay for me to go inside, to soften, to become a psychonaut, to experiment with preventive mental and physical care.

Most importantly, how do I invite other young people who think all this "health and happiness stuff" is for one kind of person, one kind of paycheck, one kind of neighborhood, and one kind of way in which they can't afford to live? How do I open the doors for them? Reach out and say: "You, too, can imagine a better world from within. If you imagine it, you can create it. Creating who and what you want to be."

"Racism is so implicit that you never even notice that it's a white girl on the cover every single time," said Amy Champ, a PhD candidate from the University of California, Davis, who wrote her dissertation on American wellness. "But when you begin to ask yourself, 'What does this have to do with my community?,' then you begin to question all these inequities."

It's funny, because we all breathe, we all move our bodies, and a ton of us pray. All the time. Bodies of culture, the global majority, we pray hard, we pray deep and loud. We pray a lot. I've seen it—my grandma was a Seventh-Day Adventist! As soon as someone would enter her home, she would spray holy water into their face, followed by a prayer for good health and good fortune. And every time you left, she'd hit you with the *"Dios te bendiga."* As a child I thought it was excessive, I thought it was embarrassing when I'd bring a friend home, and they had to be prayed over by Grandma before we could hang out.

Now I see it as courage—"to pray" comes from the French *prier*, which means "to ask"—my grandma had the courage to ask for others' well-being out loud and in public. She didn't care what you thought, she wanted the best for you. If to pray means to ask, then we are *always* praying, because we are *all* asking for things, all the time. For ourselves, for others, alone, in public, in the shower, from the universe, from the coffee place, at night, in our envy, in our dreams, in our hopes. We are always praying and asking for things.

A study in the *Journal of Religion and Health* found that 63 percent of African Americans and 50 percent of Hispanic Americans pray to improve their health, but only 17 and 12 percent, respectively, reported relying on an alternative practice like meditation or yoga to stay healthy.

My pops only recently told me: "I think it's really cool you meditate, that you're into that Buddhist stuff, you know I used to do that when I was a teenager too. I really liked it."

"Really?" I responded, "Why'd you never say anything? Why'd you stop?"

"I didn't think it mattered, and I just didn't have the time to think about that kind of stuff anymore."

I recently invited my neighbor to a meditation class with me: "Hey, Andy, come on, just try it, a drop-in pay-to-meditate class is twenty dollars. I'll cover your first one."

"Twenty dollars? I got kids to feed, bro. Time is money, and I ain't got the time for that. My rent goes up every year, and my job pays me the same."

It doesn't seem fair, and it doesn't feel good that my community, my family and friends, aren't in the marketing budget. That a preventive feel-good piece of old-school spiritual technology that can be practiced at home, in the car, at the grocery store is now expensive, elite, and highbrow.

We live in a world where imagination has become a privilege.

Where imagining something outside of our present circumstances, imagining freedom from time and worry, imagining that time spent in resting and pondering is as valuable if not more than just surviving. It's not fair that this version of spirituality is considered impossible by so many people I love.

Zen teacher, activist, and scholar David Loy writes:

> Mindfulness has actually become a tool of global capitalism. The public is persuaded that their struggles are an individual problem in need of self-help rather than a consequence of the systemic injustice many experience on a daily basis.... Mindfulness when geared towards self-help really leaves out the unjust world. When mindfulness in essence was about being awake to the unjust world.

And the world is unjust. This is a much-needed call to action. This is a desire to live as a "conscious" consumer. A desire to spend time within a community that represents the world in all its difference, not just a portion of it. If anything, meditation will give us the tools to unplug from all the consumption and plug into the conversations we really need to be having, conversations that examine issues such as cultural appropriation, sizeism, racism, ageism, classism, and happiness.

I do have an idea (and join me if you see fit): A long time ago I decided that I would always try my best to bring the teachings to the stage, the temple to the work, the Dharma to the art, the writing, the acting.

But I forgot the community. Now, I've decided to make the block my sangha (a Sanskrit word meaning "association," "company," or "community"), my studio, my place of worship, and my practice. I'm going to sit on my stoop, walk my streets with my people, and together we will sit (whether they know it or not) because we share a life that is hard, sometimes truly joyous, a life that hurts, that sustains, delights, and sometimes even protects us. I will immerse myself in the block and, in doing so, create the spirit of a world filled with accessible peace, awareness, and happiness for all. Happiness exists for all, all colors, all sizes, all creeds, each and every one of us, all. Or as the Sugar Hill Gang says it, "To the Black, to the white, the red, and the Brown, the purple and yellow." Together, we will be the universal billboard for the attainment of both happiness and coolness—because caring and actively trying to be more aware of the world's injustices and interconnectedness is cool. It's enduring, it's meaningful, it goes way beyond personal development, it changes the fucking world.

The Ameri-con Dream

"I don't read magazines, Virginia. I go to work exhausted and come home exhausted. That is how most of the people in this country function. At least people who have jobs."

—SARAH RUHL,
THE CLEAN HOUSE

I have $244,000 in student loan debt, and I went to acting school. Yes, acting school. I have a BFA in theater. I'm actually quite successful on paper, I have my own Wikipedia page, I'm a series regular on TV, I wrote a book (you're reading it), but I studied theater for four years, not brain surgery or law. And I am drowning in debt.

No one knows this (until the moment this book comes out, then everyone knows it). Not even my parents know how bad it's become, and they're cosigners on these private loans (I guess they, too, will now know).

It's not $244,000 in principal; this is what has happened with compounded interest. I owe three times as much as my original loans just in *interest*.

I signed these papers. My parents and I signed them together. My uncle came on as a cosigner, something I know he now regrets. I get it, he hates the calls, the letters, the barrage of area codes asking him for money, the fear he lives with, that if I fuck up, what little he has will all be taken away from him. It keeps him up at night. It keeps me up at night, too.

Even an ex of mine signed on as a cosigner (I actually paid this one off).

Why didn't you do scholarships or financial aid? Because most middle-class families in America are not wealthy enough to afford college but also not broke enough to be able to qualify for financial aid or scholarships. Also, I did get some scholarships—I wrote every essay you can imagine, did it cover my whole tuition? No.

Didn't you read the loan agreement? Yes, of course I read the sixty-page loan agreement with my parents sitting by my side, we all read it together—we read about FAFSAs, Master Promissory Notes, Pell grants, private, subsidized, and unsubsidized, we read through the general lack of clarity on how repayment works, and still we signed the dotted line.

Why, then? The answer is simple.

We believe(d) in the American Dream.

You know the story: "Be the first in your family to go to college, and life will be better. Be a trailblazer, and life will be better." I believed in this story, I believed in "better," and I went in search of it.

I read somewhere that Steve Jobs used to operate under the idea that once you make people believe that you have something they need, you can make them believe anything.

Why else would anyone who wasn't born into serious wealth or who received a *full* scholarship attend a private institution of any kind? Because in some way we have been conned into believing the dream, conned into thinking the more elite and expensive the college, the better the chance at succeeding. A con that is so deeply implanted into our psyche that excessively wealthy (mainly white) parents will commit outright fraud in order to win an already shitty, rigged, and skewed admission system to give their children an education that they, of all people, do not actually need. The con takes us all.

(Lori Loughlin was just sentenced to two months in prison for paying bribes of $550,000 to get her daughters into USC. Just to get them enrolled, they would still be paying tuition on top of that . . . Two months in prison. Crystal Mason, a Black mother of three children, was sentenced to five years in prison for voting when she didn't realize a past felony conviction made her ineligible. Then there's Kelly Williams-Bolar, a Black woman who was sentenced to five years imprisonment for registering her child in her father's school district. While her sentence was eventually reduced, she was left unable to complete her teaching certification.)

Do you know that episode of *Seinfeld* where George tells his recently deceased wife's family that he has a house in the Hamptons when he really doesn't? He insists on taking them there even though he knows there is no house to take them to. And the family decides to go along for this ride to the imaginary Hamptons house, even though they are fully aware that George doesn't have a house in the Hamptons, but they want to see how far this game will play out, who will break first? So they all hop in the car and insist on going on this drive to a house everyone knows doesn't exist. Everyone knows the house is a lie, but they all take the drive to nowhere anyway, they all go along with the lie and see it till its end.

That is the American Dream. We get in the car to head toward our house in the Hamptons that doesn't actually exist. But we take the drive anyway. We take it because maybe we believe in miracles? Maybe we believe a house will just appear out of thin air? Maybe we believe in the drive itself? Maybe the lie has gone so far that we can't turn back because we'll look like a fool, and nobody wants to look like a fool.

My drive consisted of me believing in myself enough to audition for the top theater conservatories in the country and getting into most of them. Then crying in the living room, when I opened the acceptance letters. Crying because I knew I had the talent to pursue my dreams, that my art wasn't just a selfish act or a bid for attention but a calling. I cried because I knew my family couldn't afford to help me go to college. They were drowning in credit card debt as it was, drowning in the mortgage and multiple home equity loans against their house.

They busted their ass daily just for us to be "middle class," just for their own slice of the American Dream; and yet there was no way they could pay for my college education. This meant that I would have to take out multiple $37,000, thirty-year private Stafford loans, for which I now have ended up paying more than $50,000 in interest on each loan. Yes, I will end up paying more interest than the actual loans themselves.

My family believed in the dream that the education I would receive would prepare me to successfully meet the needs of the world, a story that assumes that the costs to earn a degree are outweighed by the long-term benefits higher education may provide. More than anything, they believed in me. My parents wanted me to have what they didn't have. What's more of an American Dream than the hope that you can give your kids everything you never had? How many times did society say no to them? Their son would go to college because they couldn't. Their son would be an artist, because they couldn't follow their passions—my pops couldn't be the radio DJ or clarinet player he wanted to become. His parents wouldn't let him; they called those ideas stupid and pointless. My mother couldn't become the doctor she would have excelled as because she had to start supporting herself by working two jobs while in high school. Where was the time to dream and pursue a higher education?

This makes me really angry, because I saw a video of the daughter of Lori Loughlin (the woman who bribed USC for half a million) saying, "I don't really like school so I'm not excited about going to college." My parents were excited about getting an education, and that excitement was taken from them. Their son would have it different.

When I was a freshman in college, I headed home to see my family over Christmas break. I really wanted to get my parents something amazing, a gift that they would cherish, because I was so grateful for all their hard work and all they sacrificed and did for me to be in this expensive school, but also I didn't have any money.

So I decided to write them a letter. I already used all my hand-crafted IOU coupon gifts when I was fourteen, so a letter was what was left. (IOU coupons: you know the ones every kid gives their parents: the free car wash, the back rub, the head scratch, the dishes, etc.)

I worked hard on this letter. I thought, I'm going to give them this letter, and they're gonna love it, and we're all gonna keep loving one another, and it's gonna be amazing.

I read it out loud to them, the letter went something like: "Everything I do, I do for you. You sacrificed everything to give me a better life. Everything I do is to pay you back, to honor you."

I started crying, I thought it expressed what I wanted to say so clearly, and my pops's immediate response was, "Are you fucking kidding me?"

I was shocked by his response; I didn't see this coming.

My pops shook his head: "For me, don't do anything for me. I didn't do anything I did for you. Everything we've done, everything we've been able to give you, it's for us. It's because we enjoy wanting to give you what we never had. It means the world to us. So if you're going to this fancy school and you're studying acting and you're putting a lot of debt on my account for me, then save me the trouble. You do it for you, okay? For you, not me."

And I'll never forget that.

My dreams of being an artist weren't stupid to them—this is maybe the greatest gift they could have given me. They said yes to the loans, when secretly I think I wanted them to say no, knowing my battle as an artist would be an uphill one, but they said, "Yes." I would hear them late at night whispering, "Maybe our son might actually make it."

Paul George (a professional basketball player) makes $145 every second he plays basketball. Every second. That's $8.7K a minute, $104.3K every quarter, and $417.1K every game. I'm not singling out Paul George—I like Paul George, I'm a big fan of his game, he kind of crumbles in the clutch, he could help out his team more, but I still wear his basketball sneakers (they are lightweight). And he's not even the highest paid player in the

NBA, he is simply one of many athletes across many sports who can pay off my student loan debt in twenty-eight minutes or less. In less than half an hour of work I could be free from financial burden and possible ruin. And don't even get me started on their owners. Players get paid, but they also get played, too. Think of how all those white owners probably laugh at their players' salaries while not having to break a sweat or pull an Achilles to do it.

Still, I do wish I was three inches taller and blessed with better genetics, but I'm not. (*Great time to play Skee-Lo's "I Wish."*)

After I graduated, I spent that first year or so sleeping in my car. I told myself, it's a part of the journey, a rite of passage to being an artist—it's amazing the stories we tell ourselves in order to not break, in order to not lose hope. I live off of food stamps, I skip meals, I get real skinny, I pray for grocery-store gift cards, I become exceptional at sampling the build your own salad bar at Whole Foods, and every day I convince myself that it's worth it. When my mother calls me, she asks, "My sunshine, how you doing?"

"Fine," I say. "Fine." I become very intimate with the word "fine," fine as in it could be worse, it could also be better, fine.

But she can hear the truth, she can hear the tiredness in my voice, and she asks, "How are you really doing?"

I don't answer. I freeze.

My mother then cries, wishing she could do more for me.

My pops gets on the phone and says: "What do you need? I just won the lotto, for real this time, what you need?"

For years, my pops always asked me what I needed, followed by, "I just won the lotto." Always. I knew he didn't win, and I knew that if I asked them for something they would try and do whatever they could to help me. I never asked. I just said, "Fine, I'm fine, I'm fine."

When the student loans start calling every day, every hour, asking me to pay $2K a month (which is more than I and most people pay for rent, and I live in LA where rent is very high), when they start knocking on my family's door, calling them incessantly, sending letters . . . I go to more school, enrolling in a low-residency master's program for expressive arts therapy, not for the fun of it, not because I want to continue my education, but because I can't afford the monthly student loan payments, and I need to buy myself more time. Because I refuse to let student loans destroy another dream. But even "in school deferment" doesn't last forever.

My financial circumstances have changed, but that always present anxiety in the pit of my stomach is still gnawing at me. I am paying off my student loans, I might be till the day I die, and because of this I am afraid to have children. On top of coming into a world that is already not set up for them to succeed, an earth in crisis, now do I also really want to make the fight harder for them by burdening them with my outstanding debt from that time I went to college?

The federal government declared that the birthrate declined for the sixth straight year in 2020, a trend that's been building for the last decade. Wow—it's almost like a whole generation has been saddled with massive debt, then hit with multiple economic crises while living in a society that shows clearly how little they care about children or caregiving.

This fear is exactly what they wanted, right? The fear that immobilizes a young person from any sort of movement, especially upward. If everyone moved upward, would there be enough room at the top? Someone has to lose, right? Someone has to be the *also-ran*.

Also-ran. It's a term that comes from the world of horse racing, it's often used in Latinidad circles to say not everybody wins, but you need the other horses to run. You need the *also-rans*. I think somewhere deep down inside, America believes that not everybody can win or should win. That we just need some suckers to run and run and run and run and run and run and run, with just enough belief that they might win if they just run fast and hard enough. Just as important as the winners are the *also-rans*.

Show me an empire, show me an economic system not built on the backs of the oppressed, on the also-rans. To get the lavish, opulent luxury, you need cheap labor. The people hustling harder beneath you to make it happen. You need workers grinding their bodies into the ground until there's nothing left but ash and dust. Workers that work all day, every day, and don't get time off, working until they can't. Until they die. Workers who are line items on a spreadsheet, and all that matters is the bottom line.

How do you get these workers and also-rans to keep hustling, to keep running, to keep grinding? You sell them a dream. A hustle that never ends. You show them winners, not also-rans, you show them that winners are what matter in society, and that everyone else is secondary. You show them stories and fantasies where life is only good for the hustlers who gave everything to the dream. You sell them a con that doesn't exist for mostly anyone, white people included, and it especially doesn't exist for the global majority.

My story is not mine alone, I am from a generation buried in student loan debt. I have been betrayed by the dream, and yet (believe it or not) I am definitely one of the lucky ones. I'm keenly aware that I've had an exceptionally fortunate professional life and life in general. I somehow managed to keep enrolled in school while not taking myself away from auditioning and creating. I took as many deferments and forbearances as possible to just buy more time. I played the game as best as I could.

Sometimes I know I got lucky. Sure, I busted my ass. There was a shit ton of hustle and buying into the American Dream that sold me upward mobility as attainable with an ingredient as simple as hard work—and yes, any person who navigates marginalized intersections and has broken through classist, racist barriers did so with fierce persistence and working harder than their white counterparts—yes. But also, what it leaves out is some luck. To be a person of color, to navigate white supremacy and capitalism, takes both work and some luck.

If you're super lucky, if everyone likes you, you might be able to get that GoFundMe to go viral, you might end up being able to pay for your insulin, or your surgery after your biking accident, or your $170,000 hospital bill after giving birth, you might be able to pay for your education and other basic needs . . . LUCK.

My favorite tweet of 2021 was:

GoFundMe (2012): just a cool lil website where ur friends can support your projects :)
GoFundMe (2021): the backbone of the American healthcare system.

Last year I spent two days in the emergency room, the bill was $48,319.50. For two days. I am very appreciative for whatever happened in those two days that allowed me to be okay. I am beyond grateful that my insurance covered $45,305.15, leaving me with a balance of $2,965.96. I called my mom in disbelief.

"Yo Ma, they want me to pay $2,965. Why aren't they satisfied with $45K? Also, that's a lot, isn't it? I have insurance, good insurance, union insurance."

My mom said, "If you get out of a hospital with a bill less than three grand, consider yourself lucky."

Luck.

When I tore my ACL, I had surgery to replace it. The cost of that, without insurance, was somewhere close to $120,000. Luckily, I had insurance. I met a fellow Dominican entrepreneur a few weeks before my surgery, he had his own brewery in Washington Heights, it was well distributed too. He also had a torn ACL but no insurance, and he certainly couldn't afford to drop $100K to fix it, so he "decided" to just live with it.

The American Dream used to be owning a home with a white picket fence, now it's just surviving and getting out of debt.

The con is the DNA of this country.

The colonizers stole land from the Indigenous peoples and then forced them to work that stolen land against their will. "Jobs," the colonizers called them. Jobs they didn't need before white supremacy set up shop on their land. They were paid money that could only be used in colonizer stores, to buy goods they were told they needed, goods that were unnecessary before the colonizer's arrival.

They were never able to save any of this money because they needed to spend whatever currency they acquired in order to survive. It's a form of circulation at its finest. It's not regenerative by any means, but it certainly keeps the money in the right hands. You're not actually losing any money when it goes right back into your pocket.

America is the original pyramid scheme, like a college education for anyone who can't afford it outright—you borrow money from rich people to get an education that will make you more efficient at making rich people more money. Then the rich people will give you a fraction of the money you earn from them and call it a wage. Then they will demand that you use that wage to pay back the money that you owe the rich people. This is the private and public sector, it's people, it's institutions, it's everything.

It's systemic and well-curated oppression.

Right now, the US government charges an interest rate on student loans that covers the administrative costs, covers the bad-debt losses, covers the cost of funds, and then, on top of all that, makes a profit for the government. How much profit? Well, the loans that were put out between 2007 and 2012 are on target right now to produce $66 billion dollars in profits for the US government. And where is this $66 billion dollars in profit ultimately going? Not back to my pockets, not to my health care, not to the public schools that have to keep cutting staff so that there are forty kids for every one teacher, not to the planet's well-being, not to housing the homeless . . . Probably to someone's yacht, another house in the Hamptons, a private jet, and maybe a parent or two who want to bribe a university into getting their kid into a top-ranked college that the kid doesn't even really want to attend. Oh, and to war and the expansion of American colonialism.

When do you actually begin to earn? To save? When does the cycle of servitude end? The dream says, "Work long and hard enough, and you will be free." Like the enslaved people put on the front line who were promised that if they fought for us, got shot first, they would be free, land included. But we all know how easily this country takes back its promises.

A loan is just a promise, a promise I had to make if I wanted an option at reasonable social security.

And when I struggle to fulfill said promise, I feel as if I have done something wrong, as if I have failed. The anthropologist David Graeber says in his book *Debt: The First 5,000 Years*:

> If history shows anything, it is that there's no better way to justify relations founded on violence, to make such relations seem moral, than by reframing them in the language of debt—above all, because it immediately makes it seem that it's the victim who's doing something wrong.

I played by the rules, I was one of the good kids, I got great grades, I went to one of the best acting schools in the world, I did the right things, and yet where is my bailout? AIG took out contracts and made promises, airlines and Fortune 500 companies take out loans and sign major contracts, and they are not held to the same standards as poor Latino kids from Queens. They get bailed out, and I still owe them six figures, because in America not everyone has to pay their debts, only some of us.

Obama only paid off his student loans during his second term as president. After he wrote his second book. Do I have to become president to pay off my student loans?

In 2020, in the middle of the worst economic downturn since the Great Depression, where millions of families, particularly in working-class communities of color, either scraped by or fell further into debt, not being able to afford their rent or groceries, JP Morgan Chase posted one of its best quarters ever, taking in $4.7 billion in profit.

The year 2020, where more poor people died than were rich, a year where the rich actually got much richer. From March 2020 to March 2021, America's billionaires increased their combined fortunes by more than $4 trillion, according to an analysis by Americans for Tax Fairness and the Institute for Policy Studies.

After receiving billions from the government in order to stay afloat, Gary Kelly, Southwest Airlines CEO, said, "We can't deny that we are still flying because of the generosity of the American taxpayer." Whose generosity? Mine? The taxpayer who was never asked if they wanted their generosity placed in that direction in the first place?

Jeff Bezos has a net worth of $210.3 billion and growing (as of 2021), which means he could spend $1 million and buy around *$35 million* worth of student loan debts. Then forgive it. It would wipe out debt for hundreds of thousands of students and graduates for cents on the dollar. It would help revitalize the economy. He could drastically change people's lives and still have $209 billion left. John Oliver did it with medical debts, purchasing $15 million worth for just $60K! It's possible.

But no, Bezos and other billionaires are in their lairs playing Star Wars and burning 50 million tons of CO_2 per minute. Elon Musk said, "Those who attack space maybe don't realize that space represents hope for so many people."

Trust me, billionaires paying their taxes, assisting in world hunger, ending homelessness, helping the planet (which is literally on fire), and stopping people from rationing their insulin represent much more hope for many more people.

The con is what allows a thirty-seven-year-old Mark Zuckerberg, whose net worth is $126.8 billion (which means a single human has nearly five million times as much money as the median American household), to be able to single-handedly and effectively sway elections, change the way we relate to one another, and control social definitions of what is acceptable and true. Zuckerberg built his wealth off publicizing the con. The con consumes our attention: instead of focusing on free education, healthcare, fair wages, and benefits, we have our personalities, Instagram stories, likes, and retweets.

How many people do you know who went viral or pray or wish that something they do or make would go viral? Meanwhile, in 2020 a truly viral pandemic began killing and spreading at a mass rate; and during this "down time" many of my friends' talent and entertainment manager's advice to them was, "Now is a good time to build your social following."

The con is how far we will we go to pretend the system is okay, pretending that we are okay, that everything is okay—we will drive all the way to the Hamptons with our dead fiancée's parents to a house that doesn't even exist.

My pops told me to "pretend," to fake it till I make it, to do whatever I had to do until it worked. Often, to be a person of color in the world of higher education is to be so desperate to fit in that you must *pretend* to fit in by any means necessary. You pretend even if it means signing away your financial freedom (as if you actually had any to begin with).

And for some of us, it's a useful con, but for most, it sucks. It steals from us, consumes us, and punishes us for believing in it. And for people of color, society forced us to believe that the con is our only way out. I went to play the part of college student, and now I am actively playing the part of fearful adult who made a poor financial decision and now has a six-figure barrel shotgun staring down at me at all times.

Fun facts:

The student loan crisis in America is currently valued at $1.59 trillion and set to double by 2025. Education was once a government mandate, right? Now, as student debt rises, so do the seven-figure salaries of top university presidents.

Forget filing for bankruptcy, while most companies, corporations, and people can use bankruptcy to shed other debts, the rules of student debt provide that the obligations of a college loan follow a borrower to the grave. I'm afraid to die before my parents do, I don't want them to be burdened with my debt.

In Europe and Canada, you only have to pay student loans back when you make enough to cover them.

The average American student graduates with enough money in student loan debt to buy a top-of-the-line Tesla.

Ninety-nine percent of people applying for student loan forgiveness are rejected.

In 2019, of the 86,006 PSLF applicants (student loan forgiveness), only 864 received an approval.

Let's just start again and forgive the loans. What do you say? Is that unfair to all those people who struggled for years to pay back their student loans?

As David Graeber says in *Debt: The First 5,000 Years*:

> Let me assure the reader that, as someone who struggled for years to pay back his student loans and finally did so, this argument makes about as much sense as saying it would be "unfair" to a mugging victim not to mug their neighbors too.

Again, this notion of "fairness" implies that there is an equal playing field to begin with, and there isn't. Nothing has ever been fair in America.

It's obvious, the loan can never be paid back and the promise can never be truly fulfilled or the entire system would crumble, we wouldn't be so dependent on our puppeteers, we would have freedom and mobility—and freedom is not why we stole land, bodies, minds, hearts, and culture. At least not my freedom. Being debt free opens doors; the system wasn't designed for the doors to be opened for just anybody. Remember, we need the *also-rans*.

It just so happens that with the system that exists, the majority of also-rans are BIPOC, and the way that student loans are currently distributed causes much more suffering than assistance.

If a young person asked me if he should go to college, I would reply like Maggie Smith in her poem "Good Bones":

I keep this from my children. I am trying
to sell them the world. Any decent realtor,
walking you through a real shithole, chirps on
about good bones: This place could be beautiful,
right? You could make this place beautiful.

If I got to do it all over again, would I say yes? I have a college
degree, and I'll always say how special that time was for me, and
how it's served me well.

That said, I am not convinced that college is truly necessary
for everyone. There are other forms of education. There are
much cheaper forms of education. There are trade schools.
There is sometimes the benefit of just doing the work. There is
a whole infrastructure of work needed that can begin without a
college degree.

I'm not anti-education, I am against the cost of education. I
am against the mind-bending, utterly indefensible skyrocketing
cost of tuition. I am against the pressure we put on kids to borrow astronomical amounts of money at such a young age. Money
to get expensive degrees that too frequently fail to lead to a job
that will pay them enough to pay back the debt. The best path
for most people should never be the most expensive, and as long
as the government is in the business of lending billions of dollars
to young adults, I'm going to question if it's for their good or to
keep producing *also-rans*. I invite you to question and resist that
con as well.

Sacrifice My Identity. I'll Do It. I Will Do Anything to Survive.

"O my body, make of me always a man who questions!"

—FRANTZ FANON,

BLACK SKIN, WHITE MASKS

L ife is not just hard for the global majority; it is beautiful and special. It's a thing to celebrate.

It's not just "Woe is me," but "Yeah is us!"

I think young children of color need to see these messages too. I don't want this book to be another reminder of pain with no end in sight, I also want to tell you what is right, what is good, what is beautiful:

My culture has things that no other culture has. Our BIPOC cultures are rich. We have skills and flavors that exist nowhere else, we have old and deep magic that heals and restores. Me and other Brown, Black, and Indigenous bodies of culture share so much intimacy that isn't rooted in trauma and suffering.

And yet, I still can't erase the memory of being pulled out of my car multiple times late at night and harassed, made to run through test after test to see if I was troublesome, or dangerous.

I will never forget being arrested after being pulled over for texting, which I admitted to, because I was definitely writing a poem while driving down the 101 freeway, which was not safe. Even after admitting to that, after fifteen minutes of questions about where I was, what I was doing, why, after admitting guilt for using my phone and ready to receive a ticket, I was then made to get out of my car, where I was put through another thirty minutes of an officer testing me physically to see if I was drunk (I wasn't). At the thirty-minute mark, before doing another test, I asked the officer, "Can you please give me a minute?"

"Why do you need a minute?" The officer asked.

"I'm nervous," I said.

"What do you have to be nervous about? It's not like you did anything wrong."

And this, this is where my fate could have gone down a much scarier and more unfortunate road. Because I know what I said next was a mistake. A fuck up. A stupid thing to do. And on any other day it could have escalated from banter to brutality. But I was scared and I was angry, and I had spent thirty minutes already trying to do anything in order to survive. Maybe in some way what came next was me giving up, it's gonna be what it's gonna be, I thought . . .

"Let's switch places," I said. "I'll hold the gun, and then you tell me how you feel."

The officer didn't think I was funny, or smart, or clever. The officer grabbed me, spun me around, and threw my face into his car. I started to apologize profusely. "I'm sorry, I'm sorry, I didn't mean it, I'm sorry, it was a mistake, I know you're just doing your job."

I was begging, I was doing anything to walk out of there okay. Yes, I opened my mouth, and I shouldn't have. All my non-white friends scolded me: "Fuck is wrong with you!?" "Don't be an idiot." "You're lucky that's all that happened." "We can't afford to get mouthy with the cops, we can't afford to open our mouths, don't be foolish."

This wasn't tough love, this was anger at my ignorance.

But this also wasn't the first time I'd been pulled over, it wasn't the first time I'd been harassed and questioned and made to step out of my car. In Valencia where I went to college, it happened a bunch. This was the first time I asked an officer for something in return, space, time to breathe, the first time I expressed my right to boundaries and simple dignity. After this experience, I feel grateful for the other ones. No one should have to feel grateful about walking out of a police interaction without further consequences. But non-white bodies feel that all the time. "You're lucky, could have been worse" is said far too often in our communities. I'd so rather be lucky for something else. I spoke, and it was foolish. It shouldn't have to be an act of courage to just speak, but it is.

Yes, this could happen to anyone, but it doesn't. It happens to the same set of people over and over, and to the people who say, "Bullshit, life is hard for everyone," I say: "True, life is hard for everyone. White babies aren't handed a winning lottery ticket at birth, and Black babies aren't immediately put in baby prison, but while your skin color might not make your life easier, it can certainly make your life harder."

To this day, I am afraid of the police. To this day, my stomach drops every time a police car drives behind me or pulls up next to me. There is no feeling of safety between me and the police.

It doesn't matter if I've been a model citizen that day. Multiple miserable experiences with them have left a bad taste in my body. A tension that I can't ever seem to shake when around an officer. My body is heavy in fear.

My therapist tells me: "Chris, you have a fear of the unknown. You should practice getting comfortable with the unknown. It's all the unknown until you die. According to existential philosophy death is actually completion, that's when you know."

I love my therapist, but I reject this theory. To not be afraid of the unknown is privilege. To be able to walk and drive home knowing you will be fine is privilege.

Just look at Elijah McClain, the twenty-three-year-old massage therapist and musician who played violin for kittens in animal shelters in his spare time. He was walking home from the convenience store in his hometown of Aurora, Colorado, and he was wearing a ski mask, as he often did, because of his anemia and how easily that made him cold.

A passerby called 911. They reported a "suspicious person" in a ski mask. This in itself is a pandemic. The ease in which primarily white bodies will call the police against bodies of color for no other reason than their own fear, and of course their fear feels sincere, because there is an attachment to innocence that comes with the mantra of "white is right." This justification of fear subconsciously puts blame on a guilty other. Combine that with an inability to think about the consequences of their actions, and you have given rise to everything from the conquest of Indigenous lands to the imprisonment of innocent people.

Just open your NextDoor app—an app designed to be a community resource where people can connect with others who live close by, advertise events, discuss local politics, maybe even help one another out, etc. But, most of the time, the posts are racist alerts that are one step away from calling the police. I live in a very nice neighborhood in Los Angeles, and I have seen such posts as, "Be careful store owners, young African Americans are entering all the stores with clearly no intention to buy." Or, "There is a car that's been parked outside my house for quite a while, I think the driver is African American, does anyone know this person, blue Kia?" This reporting a car outside the house is very common, most of the time it's just Uber drivers waiting for their next ride.

According to an article on *The Verge,* when NextDoor decided to support the Black Lives Matter movement, some moderators were enraged.

"I would like to see NextDoor post a 'White lives matter' [post]," one moderator from Orlando, Florida, wrote. "Sometimes, we need to remember 'All lives matter!'"

White people are easily threatened, and that fear has consequences. White people are comfortable and have been trained to keep calling because they know on some level that their calls will be taken seriously, especially if they identify BIPOC as potential perpetrators of crime.

We don't have to call 911 for everything, for most things, especially when the person who called 911 told the dispatcher they didn't actually believe anyone was in danger. If no one was in danger, why call in the first place? And why would 911 and police continue to respond to these calls if there is no sign of danger? Because the police and the white people are afraid of the unknown, especially if a person of color is involved.

Officers arrived and stopped Elijah, the transcript from the body camera telling us that the first thing Elijah said was, "I have a right to go where I am going." This is true, and yet I wish Elijah knew that when officers arrive and see your colored body, your only right and best chance of survival is not your human rights, freedom, or dignity, but is to immediately placate the person who thinks you are dangerous by showing them that you are harmless. You do this by stopping, becoming timid. They want aggression so give them softness, move slowly, become complacent to their requests, and put your hands up immediately.

An officer then put his hands on Elijah and began to drag him to the ground. Again, Elijah began pleading his case and implored his supposed rights: "Let me go, no, please let me go, I am an introvert, respect my boundaries."

"Respect my boundaries." These words bring tears to my eyes every time. It is such a simple request, forcefully denied. I cry because he had the strength to say it to begin with, when lots of BIPOC are accustomed to having their boundaries violated over and over again. It was a brave request, it was a self-acknowledgment of dignity in the face of an extremely undignified moment.

Three armed officers then proceeded to restrain the 140-pound Elijah McClain using a "carotid control hold," aka a *blood choke*—yes, a blood choke—that's a sunny term. In the tape, you hear one officer yell at another officer, "Move your camera, dude!" Conscious enough to not be caught murdering someone on camera but not conscious enough to not murder someone.

One officer then yelled, "He is vomiting, he is begging, he is saying, 'I can't breathe.'" Another officer yells at Elijah: "Don't move again. If you move again, I'm calling in a dog to bite you." (Seems they brought the whole canine force out for this one.)

Elijah continues begging: "I can't breathe [how many times until these words sink in] . . . I can't breathe. Ouch, that really hurts. I'm so sorry. I don't have a gun. That's my house. I was just going home. I'm an introvert. I'm just different. That's all. I'm so sorry. I have no gun. I don't do that stuff. I don't do any fighting. Why are you attacking me? I don't even kill flies! I don't eat meat! But I don't judge people, I don't judge people who do eat meat. Forgive me. All I was trying to do was become better. I will do it. I will do anything. Sacrifice my identity. I'll do it. You all are phenomenal. You are beautiful, and I love you. Try to forgive me. I'm a mood Gemini. I'm sorry. I'm so sorry. Ow, that really hurts. You are all very strong. *Teamwork makes the dream work.* I'm sorry. I just can't breathe correctly."

He then vomits from the pressure to his chest and neck, and the officers inject him with a large dose of ketamine made for a 220-pound man. He suffers two heart attacks and becomes braindead by the time he gets to the hospital. According to a police report, the coroner could not determine the exact cause of death and therefore listed McClain's death as undetermined.

No one was charged.

It's a shitty story. It's fucking heartbreaking—they are all heartbreaking. But what really hits me this time, what really stands out to me are the words "All I was trying to do was become better. I will do it. I will do *anything. Sacrifice my identity.* I'll do it."

"I will do *anything. Sacrifice my identity.* I'll do it."

"I will do *anything. Sacrifice my identity.* I'll do it."

"I will do *anything. Sacrifice my identity.* I'll do it."

And this, this sums up what it is like to be a body of color in this world that is not made for us. We are just *trying to be better,* we are doing anything we can, often sacrificing our identities to fit in, to be accepted, to not be a threat, hated, or killed.

Whatever it is, anything, we'll do it.

If you read his last words, you see him trying over and over again to become as little of a threat as possible: from his relationship to insects, his eating habits, the fact that he doesn't judge people who do eat meat, his horoscope, *teamwork makes the dream work*. Aside from becoming as little of a threat as possible, I also think he was saying we can bond and connect in some way. I swear we aren't so different, something in me can connect to something in you.

Out of all the murders, Elijah's destroyed me. I was full of grief, grieving things and people I didn't even know needed grieving. Grief is a confusing thing: while we all go through the steps, none of us have the same experience. I feel like calling them "steps" is really misleading, it gives the illusion that coping with grief is a linear path, when in all actuality it is simultaneously juggling all your emotions at once, trying not to lose your shit.

And I so badly wanted to lose my shit. I wanted to yell at everyone. I saw myself in Elijah. How could I not? There was this sensitivity in him that I recognized in myself. He had a poet's spirit. He was an artist. He was trying to speak to these officers' hearts. His last words could be so many of our last words, regardless of skin color or background. He had faith in humanity until his very last breath, *"Teamwork makes the dream work."* That kind of faith isn't supposed to let you down. But it did. I certainly wasn't as generous with my officers as Elijah was with his, I wasn't as open to collaborate, and still, somehow, I got to walk away.

For so long Elijah was me—a person of color doing *"any-thing," "sacrificing my identity,"* anything I could to survive in this world.

Reading his words felt like I had betrayed myself, and for what? When push came to shove what would all that sacrifice, begging, and pleading do for me? All these rituals Brown, Black, and melanated folks have for staying safe in the world. It's our fear of the unknown, we think by dimming our light for white people's comfort, our safety might become known to us. White people will know we are not a threat.

It sucks to know the body is a target. To know that the flesh and hair follicles I was born with can be weaponized against me.

"The body keeps the score" is a term coined by Dutch psychiatrist and pioneering PTSD researcher Bessel van der Kolk. In his book by the same name, he explores the "extreme disconnection from the body that so many people with histories of trauma experience."

We disconnect from our bodies in order to move forward, in order to not have to confront the trauma that is surrounding us on a daily basis. We push it all down in hopes that everything will just be fine.

But we can't really hide from the trauma, because all around us the past is still very much alive. There are videos of Black people being murdered on social media, police brutalizing citizens with impunity, and all the other reminders that the system doesn't care about non-white bodies. Our bodies are constantly bombarded by warning signs.

This trauma, Van der Kolk notes, "Affects not only those who have suffered it but also those who surround them and, especially, those who love them." That is to say, you don't have to have been harassed to experience the ramifications of this trauma. The ugliness of racism and abuse is buried in our body and engraved in our DNA. Ask any woman walking home alone at night: just because nothing hasn't happened to her doesn't mean she doesn't know it can happen, and her body gets tight, maybe she puts her keys in between her knuckles, she prepares her body for confrontation. This physical tension and fear takes a toll on us all.

There are communities, neighborhoods, blocks filled with constant trauma. It takes a tremendous toll. We don't feel safe, and safety is important for so many things. Even though I fear the unknown, I believe we can't make any progress or growth unless we feel safe enough to take that next step into the unknown. Unless we feel safe enough to move forward. When we don't feel this safety, that is when cycles begin, we start to believe this trauma is all there is, this trauma is our worth, this trauma is our life. I think this is true in regards to finances, business, health, love, sex, relationships. Safety allows us to walk into those unknown spaces.

Van der Kolk writes, "Being able to feel safe with other people is probably the single most important aspect of mental health; safe connections are fundamental to meaningful and satisfying lives."

Being frightened means that you live in a body that is always on guard—an angry and defensive body. If your body already knows that you are at a disadvantage, then Elijah only spoke the truth that night: "All I was trying to do was become better. *I will do anything. Sacrifice my identity.* I'll do it."

What is needed in order for BIPOC to relax our bodies? What is needed for us to feel safe in the unknown? In order to stop trying to be better for something as basic as survival? What is needed in order for us to no longer be okay with sacrificing our identity? Elijah was saying he would be whatever the officers wanted him to be in order just to live. I also begged. I want us to stop begging.

I think all bodies of culture have done this at some point in their lives. Some macro, some micro, we have all sacrificed our identities for someone else's comfort or approval for a false sense of safety. I think this is where the power of grieving comes back into play for me. I must grieve for the times when my boundaries were not respected. I must grieve when I know I sacrificed my identity, I must grieve that I see this pattern continuing. I am not sure that safety is the immediate goal (the long-term one, yes), because maybe safety is never possible in this life, but solidarity with one's reality and oneself is.

Grieving publicly and with loved ones is one way I have found to relax and feel safe.

Another is storytelling.

Asking what stories must die so new ones can grow? It is all about turning wounds into scars. Creating new imprints with our old narratives. Language gives us the power to change ourselves and others by communicating our experiences, helping us to define and redefine what we know.

If my capacity to heal is greater than my capacity to destroy, then what destructive language can I replace with healing language? How about the violent language that lives in me? Even today after my workout I said something like I "killed" it. Or, I "murdered" it," I "slayed."

It's not only using violence to pump me up or to motivate and celebrate, it's also when I feel bad about a moment or myself, I say things like, "Just shoot me now," or "Just kill me now." "No pain, no gain" or a million other generic quotes that tell me to try harder, be more aggressive, do more, and take more.

I can't change the fact that when LA was grieving and rioting after the murder of George Floyd, and the city was given a curfew, I texted my best friend shortly after the city-mandated curfew began (btw, my parents never even gave me a curfew): "Yo, bad idea to go to a park to move my body?? Move energy. Clear my mind."

He responded quick: "You are a six-foot man of color. Stay the fuck home."

I am 6'1", but I knew exactly what he meant.

I don't know a world without violence. I don't know a world where people of color aren't disproportionately murdered without rhyme or reason. I don't know skin that isn't born running on a treadmill. I don't know a world other than this one.

I do know that the body keeps the score, and that if my Brown body keeps this unawake hypnotic commitment to violence in my own language, then they (white consciousness, white bodies, bloody history, and colonization) are winning. They get the exact mindset from me that they expect. If I maintain this commitment to violence, who or what am I serving? No one. Certainly not myself and certainly not my Brown and Black brothers and sisters who already have so much violence to contend with on a daily basis. Certainly not Elijah McClain, who was willing to sacrifice his identity for one more breath.

I pray that from now on when I do a good job, I didn't "kill it," because people I love, people who look like me are actually being killed daily. From now on when I did a good job, I "showered it with love."

I went to the park despite the warning. I went because I tend to push my luck. I went because it shouldn't have to be an act of courage to just go to a park. Above all, I went because no longer does any *body* of color deserve to be afraid to just exist.

The world is chaotic enough as it is, my participation in your violence doesn't have to be. No longer will I do anything just to survive, no longer will I sacrifice my identity. I can set myself free and decolonize from the violence in my mind and in my heart, violence that doesn't belong to me, it's not mine to hold anymore.

I hope and believe that by grieving and declaring this commitment publicly, I will be able to get a little freer from the fear and walk into the unknown.

The Real James Bond ... Was Dominican!

> "Heroes, as far as I could see, were white—and not
> merely because of the movies, but because of the land in
> which I live, of which movies are simply a reflection."
>
> — JAMES BALDWIN,
> ***THE DEVIL FINDS WORK***

I pop my head around the corner, the coast is clear. I do a fully executed tumble in a pair of tighty-whities and socks, landing in a fighting stance. I'm fully strapped—Nerf gun in my right hand, Nerf pistol in my left, a Nerf grenade launcher slung over my back. I've got a makeshift belt attached to my hip holding one more Nerf gun, while a single-shot Nerf is tucked into my socks.

I do another tumble and fire into the distance, whispering into my invisible watch (with a perfect British accent), "I'll be in and out in six flat."

I check the perimeter for my target and then check my back for people sneaking up on me before firing again. My mom yells from the kitchen: "*Coño, muchacho.* I swear, if this food gets cold, if I have to tell you one more time, I will break all your toys. *Everything.* I will break *everything*!"

I whisper again into the watch, "Ah, my bad, Bond is gonna have to meet you at the drop-off point after dinner."

"*Everything*!" my mom shouts again from the kitchen, which is only ten feet away from where I stand, but she's acting like I'm at the park across the street.

I drop the guns. "Ma, *okay*, I heard you."

"And put some clothes on!" she adds, as I undo my improvised belt and head to my room, which is really just a partitioned part of our living room, but still it's mine.

As a kid, my white friends were able to put themselves in any movie they wanted. They could fantasy cast their own biopic in a matter of minutes. They had endless choices of nearly identical celebrities and characters and stories that looked like and represented them, their food, their faces, their hair, their families, their homes, their Tuesday night dinners.

As a 4'10" prepubescent Dominican kid with glasses, a big nose, and a curly ass afro in Queens, who did I have to choose from? About three actors and three storylines that were criminalized, hypersexualized, and mediocre at best. But I wasn't tough enough to be Danny Trejo, and I wasn't sexy enough to be Antonio Banderas, so what was I to do?

I chose James Bond.

Who wouldn't wanna be Bond? He's chill, tough, everyone likes him. He does important work saving the world. And he gets mad honeys. All while rocking a ridiculous bespoke black tux. Yeah, Bond was the homie.

Even though I wasn't British (still not British) and I didn't look like anything like Pierce Brosnan (still don't look like Pierce Brosnan), Bond seemed tangible. He was just a person, a cool dude, and maybe I could actually become him one day, just with a touch of Latin flair. Bond. Jaime Bond. *Bondisimo*.

Twenty years later, I had left my Bond days behind. After taking off a couple of years between high school and college to "find myself," I decided I wanted to act full time. I auditioned for acting conservatories around the country and was admitted to the "prestigious" acting conservatory, the California Institute of the Arts. The only thing whiter than the school was the neighborhood surrounding it. Valencia is the whitest suburb of suburbs I have ever been to, a far cry from Queens.

But CalArts was perfect for me. It was a place to reinvent myself. During my four years there, people seemed interested in me in a way I'd never experienced before. I truly was the token colored person, which was not my experience in New York. I leaned into the stories they had about me. Chris, the Latin kid from Queens, was funny, loud, abrasive, suave, cool, athletic, and edgy all at the same time. And I fulfilled this role for them and maybe even myself.

Until one night when my friend Steve emailed me an article from *Vanity Fair*, with the subject line, "Yo, Rivas, check this out!"

Steve wasn't in the acting program but the very small playwriting program (they accept three playwrights a year), and he was also a fellow Latino. We met after a reading of a play he had written about his time in Cuba. After the play, we grabbed coffees from our school's vending machine (these coffees were super yummy) and talked until 4:00 a.m. I felt like Steve could see past all the facade, the trying, the pretending, the acting when I shouldn't be acting. I could just chill with Steve in an easy and effortless way.

I opened the email, clicked on the link, and I meet Porfirio Rubirosa.

Rubirosa, or "Rubi" as he was called, spoke five languages and was twice the richest man in the world. He was an international polo champion, diplomat, and treasure hunter. And he ran with every big name of the 1950s and '60s: from Frank Sinatra, Sammy Davis, Jr., and the entire Rat Pack to Meyer Lansky and Bugsy Siegel. He was in with the Las Vegas mob *and* the NYC mob. He was friends with JFK, Errol Flynn, Prince Aly Khan, Judy Garland, Marilyn Monroe, Rita Hayworth, Ava Gardner, Noel Coward, and more.

More than that, he was also Ian Fleming's inspiration for James Bond! Yes, the character I loved most as a child actually looked like me. Yes, the movies have been lying the whole time. Yes, the fourth most successful franchise in history was based on a Brown man, a Dominican man, like my father, like me.

Rubi went everywhere and was with everyone. He spent time in Hitler's Germany and Castro's Cuba, and not surprisingly, the FBI followed him for seventeen years. He had an eleven-inch…yeah! It's why the pepper grinder is named after him. You can Google it, it's okay. I'll still be here when you get back. Just be careful because the internet rabbit hole on Rubirosa is deep.

I was twenty-one years old, and I will never forget sitting at my computer, feeling like my entire world had been shattered. In a time when most Latin men were perceived as either dictators, gardeners, drug smugglers, or Ricky Ricardo, here comes this Renaissance man. Rubirosa, a Brown-skinned *Dominicano*, navigated the waters of all social cultures and places. He bathed his skin in honey, raced Ferraris, and flew B-52 bombers as a hobby (for reference, I play basketball on Tuesdays).

He lived by a code of rules: "One night out, one night in. Only drink enough to make you brave; and always, always know when to leave."

And yet this man of color, quite possibly the most interesting man in the world, had been forgotten, replaced instead by whiteness.

It made sense. Of course, Bond is Brown, of course someone with that much swagger is Dominican and Latino. If you'd met my pops, you'd understand. Bond is a natural island brother.

I stared at Steve's email again, but I didn't feel any hope or excitement. I felt despair. Because if this man can't be remembered, how will anything I do ever be enough? What would I have to be to be remembered? We remember Pablo Escobar, we remember Tony Montana (he's fictional, but you get it), and yet we erased Porfirio Rubirosa. Worse, we replaced him with Pierce Brosnan and Sean Connery—who isn't even English.

In a single instance, Brownness had found me, and it changed my life. Suddenly, I saw the lie. I saw how society, television, culture, and history had been written to recast the Brown and Black hero with someone suave as opposed to someone *muy* suave, with someone with far less melanin and a lot less *sabor*. Edward Bernays, the father of advertising and the nephew of Sigmund Freud (I think this is very connected), wrote in his book *Propaganda*: "We are governed, our minds are molded, our tastes formed, our ideas suggested, largely by men we have never heard of. . . . It is they who pull the wires which control the mind."

He knew that the secret to influencing preferences was not in advertising a product's attributes but associating a product with deeply held values, such as freedom and power.

As I read that *Vanity Fair* article, I could see the strings Edward Bernays had birthed. I understood that there is the way the world is presented and then the way it really is. This was the *first* moment in my life that I *felt* my race. Maybe I'd felt it before, I was certainly governed by it, but I didn't have any language for it. I felt its weight, its heaviness, its history. I felt my Brown skin, my nose, my hair. I felt my story and the stories put on me, and the facade began to crumble. I felt my differentness.

In that moment, I realized, sitting there in all-white, suburban Valencia (likely the screener audience for every Bond movie ever), I didn't have the same shot at playing the game because it wasn't my game to play.

I called my father and asked him if he knew about Porfirio Rubirosa.

"Of course," he told me.

I couldn't believe this. He knew? "Why didn't you tell me about him?" I asked.

"Didn't think it mattered. In fact, I haven't really thought about him in more than forty years."

"You didn't think it mattered?" I practically shouted. "This man was a big deal."

"He was a playboy—" my father began.

"He was so much more than that, Pops."

"Oh okay."

"If you don't give me someone besides Juan Luis Guerra, how can I honor our culture?"

"Sorry. I didn't think it mattered." My father remained unperturbed.

And this is the rub. Why did I have to read about Rubirosa in a *Vanity Fair* article written by a white man (no offense Gary Cohen, I'm sure you're a good dude) in order to learn that James Bond was Dominican?

I wasn't provided with this historical information, not by my mother, not by my father. I had to look that up on my own. I asked my grandma, my mom, my friends, and no one seemed to care as much as I did. No one was as shocked, moved, angered, or engaged as I was. It just wasn't a big deal to them.

I wasn't mad at my parents because I'm sure they've been working hard their whole lives to make it in America. And that meant assimilating, for better or worse. And when you're spending every day working to adopt someone else's culture, that doesn't leave you much time for extracurricular education about your own.

I just thank God neither of them lost the ability to cook up a mean *sancocho*, with some arroz and *tostones*, that they retained their love for *sazón*, and having a dance party whenever or wherever.

But it wasn't Ian Fleming's plagiarism of Rubi's life that really broke my heart. Not the accolades, the money, the marriages, the friends, the espionage, the months spent with Fleming at his Goldeneye Estate, or their time spent together at the casinos of Monte Carlo, where Rubi ordered his favorite drink, a "medium dry vodka martini, with a slice of lemon peel. Russian or Polish vodka will do. Shake it, do not stir it." Coincidence? I think not.

It was Rubi's choices.

In the 1940s, Rubi got a nose job and whitened his skin. The 1940s, this was way before he ever met Ian Fleming, way before Bond. Rubi was the only polo player covered in scarves in the blistering heat so as to stay *out* of the sun. In Rubi's unfinished memoir he wrote: "I don't whiten my skin and stay out of the sun and get a nose job because I like the look. It is simply because, you like the look."

Because Rubi knew then what is still so evident now, this world wasn't and isn't made for us. In order to be seen, we have to look like the noses and the skin of the people and places we want to be around. Why else do you think my Dominican grandmother insisted I squeeze my nose every day, multiple times, reminding me that "big noses don't get very far." She wanted me to have a chance in a world that wasn't made for noses like ours, and so every day I squeezed my nose between my fingers and pulled forward. I don't know if it did a damn thing, but I did it. I did it because I didn't think I had another option.

And yet that is the price some of us were told we had to pay. How many of us have been called "big nose" by the ones we loved? The sociologist DaShanne Stokes says, "Discrimination is discrimination, even when people claim it's tradition."

That same grandmother used to sit me down and say to me, "*Tu eres el mejor actor en todo el mundo* (You are the greatest actor in the world)." Every time I saw her. And she'd make me repeat it over and over. "*Tu eres el mejor actor en todo el mundo.*" "*Tu eres el mejor actor en todo el mundo.*"

I wanted to make her proud. I wanted to vindicate my grandmother and Rubirosa and every Brown body that had ever been forgotten, erased, with my presence on the stage. So, I applied to the prestigious schools and got accepted, believing that some-how I was worth it and that my story could balance the scales.

Rubirosa ended up drunk and dead in a ditch (yes, that is how the story ends), so how do I not end up like him? How the hell am I going to be enough? I decide to make it right the only way I know how. I dedicate myself to telling Rubi's story, writing a one-man show titled *The Real James Bond . . . Was Dominican!*

I write draft after draft the entire time I'm in college and two years after. People start calling me Rubi. I get a full-time collab-orator named Daniel Banks, who becomes part director, part role model, part therapist. I become both obsessed and haunted by Rubi's story. Daniel and this piece push me to start examining my entire life and all my choices: what I eat, drink, do, say, my love of white women, my want to please.

Rubirosa haunts me at every turn.

The first rehearsal for my one-man show is a scary morning. I've never made or shared anything like this, something so fresh and alive and almost living and breathing. I haven't slept all night; I stumble in, high on caffeine, and I tell Daniel, "Rubi spoke to me last night."

"Oh yeah," Daniel replies, humoring me. "That's a good sign, what did he say?"

"He told me to be myself."

I pause before continuing: "But not like, in the usual sense. I think he meant, be Dominican." I start to choke up. "Be Colombian, be Brown. Be honest. Not whitewash who I am or who he was."

"Look," Daniel says. Daniel is a tall, beautiful, Black Jewish gay man. When he speaks, you pay attention. "This world, its characters, and its heroes are made for the Ben Afflecks and Matt Damons, not for you, not for me, and not for Rubirosas. Christopher, this is your chance to change that."

I want to be James Bond, but I'm not Roger Moore or Daniel Craig. I'm Rubirosa. I am Dominican. I am Colombian. I am louder than the Brits, like real loud, especially during a game of dominoes, especially at a party. My coffee is sweeter and blacker. My music has more rhythm, more drums, more hips. My food is spicier. My land more biodiverse. My people are salt-air-and-sun-filled, not sun shy. I love being Brown. I think where and what I come from is beautiful, strong, fun, and yet in media and culture I have no evidence that being Brown is a good idea.

In 2019, the *New York Times* published a piece where they described Oscar and Tony winner Viola Davis as not "classically beautiful." The body of a person of color, especially a Black woman's body, is judged differently at every turn. Rubirosa knew it in the 1940s, and I know it now.

Want another internet rabbit hole? Look up images of darker-skinned celebrities and how they changed from when their careers first began. Look at their skin, their hair; once their star takes off, someone indoctrinates them, whitens them, makes them more Eurocentric, more easily relatable to the Valencia market. Not everyone but enough to take notice.

And in Valencia, melanin is an illness for which there is no cure. If a person of color wants freedom and power (which we *all* do), we must despise the thing we are. Even when we know it is what forms the best of us.

Over the years, I went from acting student to full-time actor. It's not a big stretch to play pretend for money when you've been doing it your whole life for free. But I have yet to be offered the role of Porfirio Rubirosa. Instead, I've played other inspiring parts, such as bag boy, drug dealer, landlord, immigrant, line cook, and criminal. Even if I've played some fancy drug dealers who owned hookah bars and drove Bentleys, they were drug dealers nonetheless.

I've portrayed people I would never want to become, but also I haven't had the nerve to say, "No."

Because I'm not Matt Damon enough, at least not yet. The hard part is, in order to achieve power you have to sacrifice it. Because as a man of color, my job is not to stand out but to fit in. I can't be too edgy or too soft. I need to have thick skin but not too thick. I need to be me, if only the me that fits the version pictured by Hollywood execs. But I have figured out some rules by now:

Keep the urban vernacular at a medium. Just sprinkle it in here and there. *"Yo, what's good, what's poppin'?"* But not much more than that.

Learn enough bad Spanish to keep it sexy and exotic.

Possibly change my name to Christopher Reynolds or Peter Burch.

Don't get too dark.

And relax every time someone asks me if I've auditioned for *Hamilton*.

It's surprising that I am still seeking proper representation when, according to a report by the *Hollywood Reporter*, Latinos buy more movie tickets per capita than any other group. Latinx comprise 19 percent of the US population. The screenings should be taking place in Pico Rivera, not Valencia. And yet, of the 1,300 top-grossing films from 2007 to 2019, Latinos made up only 3 percent of the lead or colead actors. For the Latino characters whose films identified their occupations, almost half—47.3 percent—were "shown in a job that did not require a specialized education (e.g., salesperson, factory worker, line cook, street vendor)."

According to the USC Annenberg Inclusion Initiative, "In the last thirteen years only two Latinx actors—Cameron Diaz and Jennifer Lopez—starred or costarred in more than one top-grossing movie"—and one of these women has played a white woman her whole career.

According to the study, which looked at 1,300 movies, which included more than 50,000 speaking characters, these were the percentages of speaking characters in films by race:

(< 0.5%) Native American, Alaska Native, or
    Native Hawaiian
(5%) Latinx
(3%) Mixed
(3.1%) Asian
(12.5%) Black
(78.1%) white

The Annenberg Inclusion Initiative described that lack of Latinos both behind and in front of the camera as "an erasure."

And yet, just last year at a rooftop party in Hollywood, a young woman said to me: "You're so lucky. You're Latin, everyone wants you right now. I'm just white. I got nothing."

At first, we both awkwardly giggled. I began to walk away. I was at a party, on a Saturday night, having fun. Did I really have to educate? Then I thought about the man I bought a piano bench from on Craigslist the other week who said to me after asking what I did for a living, "It's great they're looking for more minorities, but now I can't get a role, you know?" Or the at least a dozen people who have said to me: "You must book a bunch because no one knows what you are. Not in a rude way, don't worry, I like it."

If I don't speak up now, if I let the moment slide by into obscurity, then nothing ever changes.

I turned back to the woman and said: "My success isn't equated to luck or Brownness, those things don't trump talent and me having to bust my ass even harder than the average white person. When you say sentences like that, what you're really saying is, your only shot was racism, and now you're sad there is a little less of it. You've had centuries of *something*. Something ugly, brutal, and unfair. And well, let's be honest, you still have quite a bit, like quite a lot, like most of it."

Hollywood, where actual character descriptions read, and I quote:

"Latin or dark hair, eyes for crossover market."

"I do believe that the client would like to highlight some diversity in this role. Actor could be African American, or Latino, or a MIX of multiple ethnicities. If any actors 'able to play' caucasian are submitted, they should look potentially mixed/ethnically ambiguous. This guy is well groomed, if he has facial hair, it is manicured nicely, but not to the extreme. A clean grooming, is all."

"ETHNICALLY AMBIGUOUS OR MIXED RACE. INTERESTING & EXPRESSIVE FACE. FRIENDLY & APPROACHABLE." (Sometimes they write in all caps—is it because inclusivity and representation excites them?! Or, are they yelling, "See, we aren't racist!"?)

Hollywood, where it took three years to get three agents and two managers to understand that I am not Mexican.

Hollywood, where the only people of color cast in a film I recently auditioned for were an Indian doctor, a Spanish cook, and a Black caretaker for the white lead.

Hollywood, where I didn't get a part I was on hold for because I was more *urban* than Latin, even though the character was born in America, and it took place in New York. My managers at the time (now fired) alluded that it was my hair. "Can you try something classic," they asked, "something neutral?"

"Neutral" means racially unidentifiable. We live in a phenotype society, one where how you look is how you are perceived. So after much consideration and debate with my heart, my mind, my pride, and my management, I thought to myself, "I guess I haven't earned the right to be this ethnic yet," and I decided to chop off all my curls in favor of a crew cut.

Not far off from Rubi's style.

Sitting in that barber's chair, I thought I had to fill the slots Hollywood needed me to fill, the roles they wanted me to play. That is what people of color have been forced to do for centuries, right? We change and manipulate ourselves—our faces, our skin, our tongues—to appear more standard. We become fluent in different ways of being. When I cut my hair, I did what Rubi and many Brown people have done before me: I fell into line.

But that still wasn't enough. Eventually I also got a nose job. This is not special by any means. Not a revelation. I got it to help my acting career, and the thing that I still get hung up on is that it worked.

When I was considering the surgery, it was because my white manager at the time swore it would help. She told me to go away somewhere, leave LA for a month to get the surgery, heal, and recover. She insisted, "Rivas, everybody does it, it's not a big deal."

For the record, I have an amazing Latino manager now—you know who you are.

I asked my parents what they thought, and they didn't disagree. I made up some excuse to my partner at the time, who I was also living with, about having to suddenly go away for a month.

"Family stuff," I told her, too embarrassed to admit what I was doing, that I was erasing a part of my face, a part of where I come from. I left, changed, and after a month, I came home to LA, and I started booking work left and right. I now had evidence that looking more Eurocentric allowed me more mobility. Nothing had changed but my features, my acting skills were the same, my nose was simply thinner. I was closer to success due to embracing the Eurocentric ideal, and this made me feel further away from both success and myself.

"Success" feels counterfeit when you need to look and act a certain way to get it.

Even now, to this day, post-surgery, I still pinch my nose—in the shower, before a meeting, before an audition, before a date, on my way somewhere, in the car, today, tonight, while I'm writing this, I grab my nose between my index finger and thumb, and I pull it forward.

A friend of mine called me out on it during a coffee date: "Why do you always do that thing with your nose?"

I replied, "It's just a habit, just a thing I picked up along the way."

But what I could have said was: "It's because I've been brain-washed. It's a fear and trauma that is instilled deep within me, an ancient wound, a separation that secretly, not so secretly, makes me wish and need to look more like you."

I remember all the novellas my grandmother used to watch when we were young, and how anytime a character came on who looked like my dark-skinned grandmother, they were some sort of fool, some sort of comedy, some sort of joke. I never asked her about it, I never asked if she took notice, but remembering her words "Big noses don't get very far," she learned it from somewhere, too.

Sammy Davis, Jr., tells this story about seeing Rubi one morning at the hotel bar after a night of gallivanting. Sammy Davis is wrecked and staggering, he's got this fat headache from the night before. But Rubi, Rubi is no worse for wear. He's leaning against the bar, elegantly turned out and casually sipping a Ramos gin fizz.

Sammy asks, "How do you do it?"

"Do what Sammy?"

"Night after night and still look as if the gods chose you."

"Oh Sammy Sammy . . . Your job is being an entertainer, mine is being a playboy."

This was the morning, Sammy tells us, that Rubi taught him thirty-two different ways to kiss a woman's hand. Thirty-two. Depending on the vibe and the intention. Sometimes you maintain eye contact on the way down, sometimes on the way up, sometimes the whole way.

Personally, thirty-two ways to kiss a hand is ridiculous.

But the scene that plays over and over again in my head is that, on this day, while our two men are talking about thirty-two ways to kiss a woman's hand, everyone else they were with the night before, the entire Rat Pack, our two men's white wives, they're are all getting ready for Kennedy's inauguration. But our two men here aren't invited. In closed rooms and private yachts they are all "friends," but in public our two men of color are erased.

These characters are only seen when others want to see them.

I imagine that Rubi asks Sammy: "How do you do it? How do you, the one-eyed-Negrito-Puertoriqueño-Jew swallow it all? Frank and Dean, who are supposed to be your friends, bring out a Black stool, because they don't want you sitting on a white one. They constantly humiliate you, how do you swallow it? Why?"

I imagine Sammy says: "You know why. You absolutely know why. We don't have another option, do we? Now Rubi, repeat after me, keep your head up, keep cool, and smile. Keep your head up, keep cool, and smile."

Rubi, like me, like many Brown people, was so taken by whiteness that eventually whiteness consumed him, disappeared him. There's actually a word for this kind of thing—when a certain experience, often an experience of someone of color gets erased from storytelling. It's called "symbolic annihilation." If it sounds intense, it's because it is. Which is worse, being stereotyped or not being represented? And the answer is, both suck. Both are shitty. And Rubi, he never even got to have a say in how his story would be told.

Why is he not a part of the lineage and the legacy of the stories that keep getting swapped out by the same (white) people who are writing these biographies over and over and over again? Writing and rewriting and layering almost to justify or fortify the symbols that explain history. How many incredible figures are we overlooking? And why?

Because even after all that masterful pretending, today Rubirosa doesn't exist, his very essence was stolen. Is that what is happening to me? Am I too busy pretending, keeping my head up, keeping cool, and smiling that I am in danger of letting whiteness walk off with my joy, my peace, my sense of dignity and self-love? Will I ever be able to say, "I have a beautiful body, in its original form"?

I'm just doing my best to survive. In the jungles, you find your pack. In prison, you find the ones who will protect you. In Hollywood, if you look as ethnically ambiguous as me and you want to play the game, you have to know the rules. That means code-switching, staying out of the sun, calming your curls, and keeping that nose just narrow enough. It's all part of our survival.

And survival is bleak sometimes. But so is its opposite.

Rubi sold his Brownness over and over again, killing himself by driving his car into a tree at 95 miles an hour because it was never enough. The steering column crushed his chest. and he died of suffocation, pressed to his limit with nothing left to give.

If you are reading this and you still think the color of Bond doesn't matter, remember that when we even thought about casting Idris Elba as the next 007, the world went crazy because clearly Bond matters—and a white Bond matters most.

Because the images we put on screens matter. A lot. Our brains are wired for visuals, which is why seeing comes before words. The child recognizes an image before he or she can name it. Half of the nerve fibers in our brains are linked to our vision, and when our eyes are open, vision accounts for two-thirds of the electrical activity in the brain. Since the beginning of time, images play a central role in the way that humans have learned to make sense of the world.

The images that we expose people to are the material from which they craft their sense of self. Sure, family is involved, too, but where does family get it from? Stories that are told intergenerationally, and in a society saturated by media, the information that you get or not get determining how you understand yourself and others. So, if I am a little Brown boy and I don't see myself anywhere and I don't see any story that pertains to my life or my history, I'm going to get the message that I don't exist, I don't matter, and I don't belong.

I took a scriptwriting class, and what I learned is a bit disheartening. The longevity of a show is built on the idea that its characters can never really change. For the most part lead characters need to remain self-sabotaging and can never truly grow because then the show would change, and for the most part TV executives are not the most creative, and when characters change, shows often end. This is what we are shoving into people's brains—the image that we are meant to be stuck in cycles. Meant to be trapped by our delusions, poor habits, old stories, old clichés, old abuses, old dogmas, old oppressions, and that that's okay.

It's not.

We must begin to ask what images and stories have been placed deep into our minds around race and humanity, rights and fairness. What screens, billboards, movies, novellas, and narratives have we been fed since the day we were born? For so long, Hollywood has denied people of color any depth, authenticity, and meaning because the only way you make a thousand movies a year is that you have to have a certain level of automation, and cliché stereotypes are part of that automation. Think about what would happen to the industry if it actually produced films that were nuanced, complex, and honest, they couldn't make that many at that rate.

Imagine if every script session started with: "Does this story help bring humanity into that safe and just space? Does this story marginalize an already marginalized community? Is this story true? Does this person have to be white? Does this story represent society and race and class in an honest way? Does this story help us see and imagine a new, more cooperative loving world?" Then less scripts would be approved. And that's great.

This reimagining must begin behind the camera first, because we can't be authentic in our storytelling if we're not being honest about who is telling these stories. Casting up front will not change who is signing the checks. I often use Ava DuVernay as an example. She exclusively hires women to direct *Queen Sugar*. It didn't matter if they had representation or if they were in the DGA, she hired from a pool of independent filmmakers with whose work she was familiar. As a result, a lot of them got representation, got into the DGA, and directed other TV shows after that series.

That is how you do it. She didn't form an organization or sit on a bunch of panels to talk about inclusion and authenticity. She just committed to hiring women.

It is time to create new pictures, new images, and new stories, because groups who are in power do not give up power, it must be taken, reimagined, and/or shifted somewhere else. Rewriting the narrative for people of color inevitably means divesting from the white world and the white stories and the white storytellers and the white imaginations that previously defined it. Imagine content where nothing about being a person of color is an eye-opener. A story or movie where a person of color as the lead is not a revelation or relevant to the storyline.

I don't need another stereotypical Indian doctor on TV. Another Indigenous person who is struggling on the reservation. I don't need more stories about cross-cultural first-generation conflict, and other tired clichés that sell our stories as novelties. At the same time, I'm tired of diluted stories that point to assimilation as the answer to all our problems. Color blind casting is still the recycling of old stories. I need Hollywood to make it commonplace for Black lives to matter and for any who isn't white to be anything they want to be, anything they can imagine. Common and not special. Ordinary, not extraordinary, to see a Colombian blockbuster based on cumbia-loving superheroes and not cocaine, an Afro-Dominican futurist fantasy with a bachata score, an Indian and Puerto Rican bromance buddy comedy, two second-generation South Asian kids saving the planet, a meet-cute romance drama about two young Cambodian-American kids in college, where the Egyptian leads are just hanging out and talking and not being particularly epic or making everything about race. Imagine if that was just commonplace, not exceptional, not a big deal, not the reason to make the movie, it just was.

William Blake called imagination the "divine vision." It involves all the senses, it involves everything, the body, the speech, and the mind. I believe in the media's power to start showing me something divinely different, so we can begin to imagine a new future.

The TV used to be a sign of everything that wanted to erase me, and now I am a series regular on a network sitcom. On that same TV I watched with so much awe as a child. It's pretty amazing. In one way, all the late-night studying, watching, pretending, and masking worked. I have been invited to have dinner with the gods on Olympus. Though I must continue to ask, am I just a guest, who can be uninvited as quickly as he was brought in? Or am I an equal?

My goal has always been to use Hollywood as a vehicle, understanding the use of my masks, my ambiguity, and my invitation to the table, and using that to get to a place where I could create the art I wanted to create, say the things I wanted to say, and hopefully help uplift others in telling their stories. It's nice to receive checks, but the real power is in being able to sign those checks, and nothing changes until the people signing checks begin to look a lot different, a little less old-straight-white-male and a little more of anything else.

It's not about ticking boxes and making sure people of color are cast. It's about honoring the stories that allow these people to be so magnanimous, so worthy of being more than a device for your small-minded white stories. If we looked beyond checking boxes and actually began telling stories that represent what culture is, we might begin to see that.

I don't know what's next for my career, maybe acknowledging that is the first step. *Dique*, whatever it is, I will live it to the fullest. Because that is the truest meaning of being Latino, Brown, Colombian, Afro-Latino, Dominican. It means living life to the fullest, it's in our food, it's in our merengue, it's in the way we love one another.

Langston Hughes wrote something in honor of Rubirosa after he died: "I am all for colorful gentleman of color adding color and excitement, romance and the light touch to this rather grim world of wars, poverty and racism in which we live."

I don't have answers, but I'm ready to have conversations about the deep roots of colorism, featurism, texturism, European beauty standards, and self-hate, how we live in a society that devalues magical beautiful melanin. And if one day shit really pops off, and Hollywood asks me to play James Bond, I'd say yes in a heartbeat. Yo, I got a lot of student loans.

But my Bond is Brown. My Bond is Jaime Bond . . . Bondisimo.

Home

"I admit that for me love goes deeper than the struggle,
or maybe what I mean is, love is the deeper struggle."

—JULIA ALVAREZ,

IN THE TIME OF BUTTERFLIES

It's 2019. I'm in San Francisco, sitting in a coworking space with eight strangers, taking an eight-hour workshop about death. We're talking about dying, meditating on dying, imagining our own deaths, the deaths of our loved ones, asking ourselves how we want to die, where we want to die, wondering if we're ready to die. We are attempting to get comfortable with the fact that death *is* coming, that it truly is the only guarantee. And though none of us have a terminal illness, we are preparing for it—financially, spiritually, physically.

The facilitator shares a poem with us by Jeff Foster, properly titled "You Will Lose Everything":

> You will lose everything. Your money, your power, your fame, your success, perhaps even your memories. Your looks will go. Loved ones will die. Your body will fall

apart. Everything that seems permanent is impermanent and will be smashed. Experience will gradually, or not so gradually, strip away everything that it can strip away. Waking up means facing this reality with open eyes and no longer turning away. . . . Loss has already transfigured your life into an altar.

Fuck. It's July 2020 now. And I'm reading this poem again as I take a flight from Los Angeles to Miami. We're in the middle of a global pandemic. I look around the American Airlines plane, and it is packed. I mean packed, no empty seats, no middle seats left empty by the airline, which I thought was mandatory. There are no temperature checks before we get on, no screenings, nothing.

But I am prepared for this, I'm flying in a full hazmat suit. I ordered a pack of twenty right when the pandemic started, feeling like it would come in handy. But people are looking at me like I'm the crazy one (let's not even get into how many of them keep pulling down their masks). I mean, I did accessorize the suit with white Chucks and a fanny pack. You think people would have more taste. But there I sit, breathing recirculated air through my face mask, wondering why I am leaving one epicenter of the pandemic for another.

The answer is simple: family.

Like all Latin snowbirds, my parents flew south after years of cold and shoveling snow. I haven't seen them in almost a year, and I miss them more than I have in the last twenty. The world feels like it's on fire, and my first instinct, my best instinct, is to go home.

Besides, Los Angeles is a wreck, and my mind and mental health are even worse.

The last year leading up to the pandemic was an amazing year for me. I was finally "successful." I earned a lot, my Instagram was popping, my life on paper and in those little social media boxes looked to be almost perfect. And yet every day I would wake up with this pit in my stomach. No matter my bank statement, no matter what I was doing, it was there. I tried to blame it on Hollywood, I tried to blame it on Ian Fleming, I tried to blame it on race, I tried to blame it on my skin, my hair, my nose, I tried to blame it on something, anything, anyone.

But I kept repeating the mantra "There is no greater nightmare than getting to the place you always wanted to be and finding that it's nothing like what you thought it was."

Because no matter how close it felt like I was coming to everything I wanted, every day I woke up asking: "What's next? What's next? Yeah, sure, that's great and all, but what's next?" And it was never enough. And then the pandemic came. In one day, I lost a handful of the biggest jobs of my career:

1. My first lead on a TV show never ended up shooting; it got scrapped because it needed a live studio audience. I even had my own parking spot on the Warner Brothers lot.
2. Two international speaking gigs at large festivals.
3. A TV job in New York.
4. A workshop of a new play I was developing.
5. And the chance to do my one-man show *The Real James Bond* on a multiple city tour.

I went from almost making more money than all the money I'd earned in my life to praying that my unemployment would go through. On top of a global health crisis, there were massive protests everywhere, with especially large and intense ones in Los Angeles.

All over the city there are people gathering in the name of justice, and in response the city has mandated curfews. There is an endless buzz of metal birds flying overhead, and police, riot gear, sirens, looting, anger, and rage are spilling over and into the streets.

I fell apart. I had a three-day panic attack. There is a small chance I might have had a mini heart attack.

After George Floyd was murdered and the protesting first started, my partner was telling me about how vital it was that we be out there joining the forces. I told her with very little compassion in my voice: "Protesting has happened before. It has. If it ain't George, Breonna, Ahmaud, Elijah, the hundreds that came before, it'll be another, is another, every day, most not on camera."

She didn't like this answer. She found it cold and unkind. That's fair, maybe it was. I wasn't hopeful, still hard to be hopeful when yet again Jacob Blake, an unarmed Black man, was shot in the back at point blank seven times in front of his children. Was the officer arrested? No.

It's hard to be hopeful.

And with each passing day I felt more and more tiny and insignificant. Nothing I could do or say would change the blatant racism, greed, hate, rage, hurt, oppression, and inequality toward bodies of color in this country.

In Buddhism, the universe is described as an ocean of pain and suffering. An ocean in which we are all residing, at all times.

If a truly global pandemic, and its massive injustices, have revealed anything, it's that we might be in the same ocean, but we have very different boats! Some of y'all have yachts, some of us got ferries, and most of us have logs and branches onto which we are barely hanging.

White people talk about how they don't feel safe in cities, so they start fleeing to the suburbs (white flight all over again). They harp on the dangers of protest and rioting and looting. Look, I don't like seeing people breaking up or smashing windows either, but more importantly, I don't like seeing a country looting its civilians every single fucking day.

I don't like seeing our prison system loot from Brown and Black people for minor offenses. I don't like seeing big corporations and Wall Street legally looting people like you and me. I don't like seeing looting in the form of predatory loans. I don't like the way car insurance companies loot from the poor by selling them something that gives them nothing in a time of true need. I don't like military recruiters hanging outside of low-income high schools, looting kids' dreams and possibilities, telling them that this is the only way. I don't like the way brands and music loot from bodies of culture and then sell it back to us as though we weren't the origin.

It's hard to be hopeful.

When I wasn't stewing in anger, I was on Instagram. I spent hours on Instagram. I told myself I was spending that much time online because it kept me up to date on protest locations, ways in which I could share information, and gave me access to fill out prewritten emails that demanded policy change and that the necessary arrests be made—because we all know how successful online petitions and prewritten emails are.

But what I really got into was buying shit. Instagram has become the modern version of QVC, grabbing people late at night as they shop in front of the blue light of their screen. I bought two pairs of shoes (which are STILL in their boxes, haven't been worn once), one incense holder, a new pot for cooking, a bread knife. I bought a hefty amount of books, and a *whole* lot of clothes—a Sade T-shirt (which I don't regret because Sade is queen), two pairs of pants, six pairs of underwear, one hoodie, two long-sleeve shirts, two button-downs, and two classic tees. And I just received three pieces of gold jewelry I don't even remember ordering (some real, some plated).

Before this pandemic, I had never bought one item of clothing online, but look at me now! And yet I knew why. I bought shit—low-quality manufactured shit, likely made by poorly paid factory workers in a foreign country, that will fall apart after just a few wears—as a way of hanging onto my self.

My self. My actual sense of self.

It's hard to be hopeful.

Sitting in my living room with my partner surrounded by all this stuff, drinking my third glass of orange wine because natural wine is another thing I got really into during pandemic, I spew out: "*Nena*, without the things I do, who am I? Without the Hollywood things, the speaking gigs, the performing, the mask, the roles, the places, the coffeeshops, what am I? What's the point?"

"It's just a pause," Esme says naively. "It's only for a couple months." Remember when we actually thought this would only be a couple of months?

"A pause I didn't ask for," I argue. "I feel like I'm in a workout class, and we're all holding plank, and the teacher says, 'If anyone drops this plank, we're all holding it for fifteen more seconds!' And the dude next to me drops it, and she catches him, and she says, 'Okay, fifteen more seconds!' And all I can think is, 'Yo, my dude, why am I suffering for your inability to hold a plank?' I feel like the world dropped the plank, and I'm stuck holding this position for the longest never-ending fifteen seconds of my life."

"I get that, Chris. But it doesn't explain why there are fifteen boxes in this living room right now."

She's right, it doesn't, but that's capitalism at its finest. Capitalism tells me to buy things to be the thing I think I should be, to keep participating in the story and in a system that doesn't actually care about me or my Brown body.

"Let's go protest," she says. "It'll take your mind off things. It'll feel good."

She's wrong. It'll make me feel worse. It'll remind me of the things I'm trying to numb out by buying things, lamenting the loss of things, marching for a change that I don't actually see coming anytime soon. Being numb is a dangerous thing because you just don't care about anything anymore. I don't want that to happen to me. Sure, I can believe in solidarity, but really I think it's pitchforks and torches time. I think it's monks burning themselves alive just to be seen, just to be heard and understood. I think nothing will truly change until a *white body* strapped in a bomb goes full jihad, running up to city hall and blowing itself up on behalf of everyone else that isn't white! Who will make that sacrifice on our behalf? Because people of color can't do it. Acting violent is exactly what you expect of us, is exactly how you have portrayed us since the beginning of time.

I imagine myself telling her this, but instead I have another panic attack.

My partner tries to help, but as the world's falling apart, so are we. At first we try to blame it on the pandemic, but it's not about that, it's just the relationship. A few days later, we're in her apartment in Echo Park, sitting on the couch, the space between us larger than the actual space between us. I tell her out of nowhere, "I'm flying to Miami."

"Okay, for how long?" she asks. Sirens and helicopters blare outside as though we're in a movie.

"I don't know. I got a one-way ticket."

"Oh, you got your ticket already?" She is surprised.

"I did."

"Okay, maybe I'll come visit you in a little?"

I feel like we both know the answer to this. "I don't know," I finally mutter.

This is about the time that I start receiving multiple emails a week from white companies offering me a lot of money to help them craft "We aren't racist" statements. Asking a person of color to consult you on how to tell the world how not racist you are is the epitome of the fart game. You know, if you smelt it you dealt it? White companies smelt their own racist fart, and now they wanna act like they didn't smell it. And on top of it, they're asking people of culture to come in and fumigate the place.

I delete my Instagram (I've now undeleted and reinstalled it at least fifty times since then; it's an ongoing battle) as a way of saying fuck you to resharing and prewritten emails. Fuck you to white companies asking me to do their work. Fuck you to protest without action. Fuck you to allyship. Fuck you to words with no weight. Fuck you to capitalism and buying things I don't need just to feel like I am alive.

Finally, I land in Miami. I take off my hazmat suit and throw it in the trash. I drink water for the first time in six hours, and I feel like I can breathe for the first time in years. I don't hear any sirens or any helicopters. I'm not fighting myself, my mind, or my partner. Miami feels quiet.

My mom picks me up despite being at risk. As she tells me before I arrive, "To see you as soon as possible, it's worth it."

I give her a fat hug. I want to cry, but I don't. We don't talk much in the car. My mom is a "Chris whisperer"—she always knows where I am and what I need. She drives, she holds space, we share the occasional glance, and it's really nice. It's quiet.

I begin to unwind and relax in ways I haven't in years.

My parents' home in Miami is nice. It's got lots of windows, great light, a *saltwater* pool. And after twenty years, I finally have my own room with a door.

My days consist of my parents heading off to work and me waking up when I want. I do some of my morning rituals, mediation, prayer, reading, and then I swim. I swim and read and swim and read. It feels like summer vacation. My dad comes home every day for lunch and tells me stories about his life I've never heard before, or rather I never made the space to listen to.

Over Cuban sandwiches, una cerveza, and a Cafecito, he shares the wisdom inside of him. How many times he moved as a kid, all the instability, all the high schools he got kicked out of for being too aggressive. He tells me about the men his mother was seeing who beat him and treated him like shit and how she never said anything, choosing rent over her son.

He tells me about the place and the moment when he finally found himself. He was in a high school where things were finally going well. He started playing the clarinet, and he loved it, and he was good, too. His mother had been dating and living with the superintendent of the Dakota Building in Central Park West, the same building where John Lennon lived and was shot.

"I loved that building," he tells me while chewing on a Cuban sandwich. "That's the first place I really started to notice how successful white people carry themselves differently in the world. It's kind of like they're floating. Part of it is them being oblivious to the world, part of it is they aren't afraid to make a mistake."

He takes a sip of his beer as he continues: "At first, I got asked almost every day in that building if I lived there, and it really pissed me off . . . but I didn't let them see it. Instead, I started to gain a secret, a confidence on how to move through the world. I walked with that confidence until I never got asked again. I walked like I belonged there. Because I did . . . I think I passed that down to you."

"Nah, that's all just me," I say jokingly.

After my lunchtime story sessions with Pops, my sister brings my nephew over in the afternoons, and we play some cards (at first, I let him win, and then he's actually just straight up winning). Sometimes, we play some soccer or basketball. Some days we go for a swim. Then everyone gets home, and we all just chill. We watch a movie together. We laugh, dance, be silly. It's fun, it's easy. I don't feel rushed. I'm not asking, "What's next?" In fact, for the first time in years, I don't even wonder what's happening tomorrow. Because I know, more reading, more swimming, more time with my family.

I wonder if this is how we were always meant to live.

My meditation teacher tells me, "We are never more selfish than when things aren't going our way." For the first few months of the pandemic, all I could see was what I had lost: my jobs, that big, fat paycheck, possibly even my career. We were all experiencing this great collective anguish, and I could not see outside of me.

But in Miami, I see how much of that old life was killing me. Because I had gotten everything I wanted—the jobs, the cool apartment, the partner, the Wikipedia page—and none of it felt like home. I haven't spent more than two weeks with my family in more than twelve years, but now I am spending months. I celebrate my thirty-third birthday with them. My mom wanted it to be *ultra special* since for the first time in over a decade, the family was all together for my birthday. She was furious that we couldn't go to a restaurant, even though I told her, "There isn't a restaurant in this city that cooks the way you do."

"Noted," she said. "But this one is special."

My mom proceeds to make me the best soup in the world, and soup is my favorite food. Fabada, a Spanish stew of white beans and pork. This soup on my birthday, surrounded by my family and a good competitive game of 500 rummy, in the middle of a pandemic.

Life is magic.

I might have been practicing Buddhist meditation for years, but now, here in Miami, in the middle of the craziest year of our lives, I am present. I'm with people for whom I don't have to be anything other than what I am. Fully consumed and fully present with the people I love.

At another lunch date with my pops, over high-priced fancy bowls of grains and greens, my pops confesses to me that most of his life, maybe all of it, he has been trying to prove his biological father wrong, to prove that he wouldn't turn into a junkie, into an addict, into a piece of shit, homeless, with nothing, found dead on the street.

His heart wide open, he says: "Chris, every time I look at you, I look at my life, my family, my wife, your sister, my grandson, our home, I know I made it. I know he's wrong. It's nice not to prove anything to anyone anymore."

And right when I think he's about to break and the floodgates are going to open, he digs his fork into the bowl. "This black rice is amazing. Why it costs two dollars more, I don't know. But damn it's good."

After a couple of weeks, my partner checks in with me, asking, "How about I come visit you?"

Even though I feel like a dick, I tell her, "I don't think that's necessary."

And so we break up. I begin writing and creating from a place of honesty, not a place of "How will I sell this?" or "Who will buy this?" I am writing just to write, creating just to create. I am taking action independent of outcome, because action is the thing that matters, action is the thing, not the result, the action. I am enjoying myself, enjoying my company, enjoying my presence. Doing things that brought me joy, joy for joy's sake. They aren't about being better or attaining things or bringing me closer to my goals.

And then an audition pops up in my email, and my commercial agent calls me. Doesn't really ask how I'm doing. Just tries to hype me up on how wonderful it is that auditions are happening again. Is it wonderful? I want to hang up, I want to tell him: "I don't need to be shooting a Buick commercial right now. It's not gonna help anyone or anything. I'm gonna pass."

But I don't say shit. Instead, I tell him I'll get it done. It's this pull that Hollywood has on me, its voice deep in my gut screaming, "What are you without me?"

I'm in the living room trying to jerry-rig a tripod together, when my pops walks in: "You alright? You need help?"

I do, but at thirty-three I still haven't really learned how to ask for it.

"You know, ever since this audition came through, you been in a pretty shitty mood," my pops says.

"Yeah, I know."

"Then don't do it. I haven't seen you this happy in a long time. Chris, don't lose your happiness for a Buick."

"Don't lose your happiness for a Buick." Make that the new corporate slogan.

And so, I pass. I email my agent and tell him, "I'll email you when I'm ready to audition again." I can feel the claws of Hollywood and FONMI (fear of not making it) trying to dig deeper into me, and so I read and reread that Jeff Foster poem:

You will lose everything. Your money, your power, your fame, your success, perhaps even your memories. Your looks will go. Loved ones will die. Your body will fall apart. Everything that seems permanent is impermanent and will be smashed. Experience will gradually, or not so gradually, strip away everything that it can strip away. Waking up means facing this reality with open eyes and

no longer turning away. . . . Loss has already transfigured
your life into an altar.

I read that poem every day. Every morning and every night.
Just because the kettle always boils doesn't mean it'll boil today. Anything can happen, at any moment, what really matters
when it all comes crashing down? Because it can at any moment.
It already has.

I want to know that I am safe. I want my loved ones to be safe.
I want all people to be safe to be themselves. I have no idea what
it will take for one person to recognize another. To know that
when one person suffers in this ocean of pain, we all suffer. Easy
to say, hard to feel, because the human napping on the yacht
doesn't see the one hanging on to that branch with all they got.

And then, like that, it's time to go home back to LA. I know
that I have to figure out what I'm doing with my apartment. I
need to have that now overdue conversation with my former
partner, the one where we dissect what went wrong and decide
whether the breakup is permanent or just some weird necessity
of the pandemic. I have to return to LA, banged up and boarded
up, such a far cry from the city I have come to know and even at
times love.

When I was leaving Miami, everyone cried, everyone except
my father and me. He decided not to take me to the airport, saying he had to go to work. But on the road to the airport I got a
text from him saying: "I'm sorry, I had such a good time with
you, I couldn't bear to see you go again. I decided to work, but
really I just cried in my car for the last thirty minutes. Love you,
mijo, I miss you already."

James Baldwin once said, "The great plight of man is man's inability to imagine another man."

Imagine their existence, their pain, and their struggles. To actually *feel* it. We lack the imagination. We are living in a genocide of imagination. There is so much information and so many ways to escape our boredom and our confusion and our loneliness, we lack the creativity that drives empathy. We don't have the time to care about anything else but ourselves.

And in turn, we can't feel the grief of others. We can't feel the grief of our planet. We can't feel the burning. We can't feel the starving. We can't feel the struggle. We can't feel a Black father who has to explain to his son: "When a cop pulls you over, shut up or die. Do what they say or die. Hands up, smile, head up, no sudden movements or die." We can't feel the weight of that conversation. We can't feel our own fathers until we go home and finally listen.

Remembering this ocean of suffering that we all exist in isn't about guilt, it's a simple practice to engage our imaginations in something other than ourselves. To begin to try and feel another's existence. If anything, that's why I believe in art. Because it reminds us—wow, everyone is just doing their best to survive.

My pops's favorite line to me is "Your day will come." As far back as I can remember, he has been hitting me with "You'll see, your day will come, you'll see, your day will come." If I ever do anything rude or remotely disrespectful, he smiles, a big fat smile, and says, "You'll see, your day will come, you'll see, your day will come."

During one of our many lunches together, he says: "Chris, everyone's day comes, no one can escape what's coming for them, no one. Just because white parents don't have to explain to their children about the cops doesn't mean their day won't come. Just because white people don't tighten their breath when an officer drives behind them, just because when they walk into a room and everyone looks like them, doesn't mean their day won't come. You'll see, everyone's day comes."

Or as Jeff Foster so beautifully puts it, "Everything will be smashed." Everything.

The Gospel of
Endless Growth

"If I lose my direction, I have to look for the
North Star, and I go to the north. That does not
mean that I expect to arrive at the North Star.
I just want to go in that direction."

—THICH NHAT HANH,
BEING PEACE

The first time I saw a Redwood in Big Sur, California, I
knew it was singular. Redwoods precede the naming of
places. A tree older than walls, borders, older than government and its institutions. A tree older than racism, colonialism, student loans, poor healthcare, GoFundMe, Bitcoin, debt,
Proud Boys . . . A tree older than America. A three-hundred-foot-tall tree older than all of that.

The first time I saw one I knew it was the closest thing to the
dinosaurs that I was ever going to get to. It was as if the earth
started on that Big Sur coast, as if life crawled out of the waters
right there and made a home in that forest, in those trees. I knew
it was magical, majestic, wondrous. Above all I wished I could
give it to everyone I knew back home. I knew if they were here,
standing in this grove, surrounded by thousands of years of life
and resilience that they, too, would be able to *feel* it. Feel what is

mostly indescribable, feel what must be felt—a medicine that is an ancient tree and the smell of dirt, pine, and time.

Unlike many of my friends, I never grew up camping. As an urban dweller, I didn't have a relationship to nature. I had Central Park, but I never saw or felt trees like this. Growing up a young hooligan in Queens, the closest thing I had to grandeur and magnificence (and it was magnificent) were the giant buildings I was trained to never look up at (tourists look up, New Yorkers, we just keep walking, and fast) and the bright and always-on lights of Time Square and the subway cars that kept it all going. But it was the trees, logging, and wood of Big Sur (and many more forests) that paved the way for the infrastructure that allowed so much of the urban environment in which I was raised.

I was taken to Big Sur by a college friend of mine who was a filmmaker working on a documentary about the destruction and deforestation of the Redwoods titled *This Is Why We Can't Have Nice Things*.

He was struggling to make the film, he thought it never felt strong enough to make an audience feel this tree's monumental importance. He'd say: "I can tell you that there is less than 4 percent of the original Redwood Forest remaining. I can show you exact figures for its carbon sequestration powers, but how can I make you feel how that's going to impact your father, your sister, all the people you care about? It will. It already is."

Standing underneath a Redwood named Stout, also known as Big Tree, I felt the kind of overwhelming sadness and rage that weighs down your entire body and applies pressure to your chest and claws its way to the pit of your stomach. I wanted to apologize to Stout, to all the trees that feed, protect, offer shelter, and ask for nothing in return. *I'm sorry, I'm sorry I didn't*

know better, you treat me with nothing but kindness, and I con-
sume it, I consume it all. I'm sorry for all the times I littered, for
all the times I made excuses, for anything that hurt this place, this
earth, you. I'm so sorry.

I had never thought this way before about nature or the environment. All I knew about environmentalism was "don't lit-
ter," and I only knew that because I saw my pops get pulled over
for throwing some trash out of his window and complaining
about how expensive that ticket was. I had been to church as a
child, and yet nothing felt this holy. Nothing spoke this loud
while simultaneously being this quiet, three thousand years of
existence will do that to you—it will teach you how to just be
present, how to just hold space.

I cried. My friend said, "It'll do that to you." I was a grown
man, and it's like I'd never seen a tree before. When we see it, we
can feel it. When we can feel it, we can care about it.

I don't want to lead you down the wrong path. I mean, I'm
pretty sure you know this by now, but I am no climate activist,
nor am I a genealogist, climatologist, or environmentalist. I am
a writer who recycles like your average person, I try to cut down
on single-use plastic, but mainly I have a ton of plastic waste (I
shop at Trader Joe's), I use the occasional reusable item (I did
just purchase a reusable cotton swab—it sucks though, just not
as satisfying) and grocery bag (when I remember). I do not com-
post, and I order things online all the time, more than I like to
admit. I am definitely an Amazon Prime member. I own a bike,
but also I have a car that uses gas. I drive a lot. My carbon foot-
print is large, not the largest, but large. Because it is a blurry line
between convenience and doing what's right. I live in that little
piece of time that I call mine, but that piece of time is not only

my own life, it is the summing up of all other lives that are simultaneous with mine. Yours. Ours.

What does this have to do with Brownness? Everything. If we can't care for one another, then we can't care for this planet, and if we can't care for this planet, then we can't care for one another, we can't care for our neighbors or our block. Not as I'm throwing trash on the street or ignoring the fact that at the same exact moment that I watch a gorgeous food documentary on Netflix, there are three homeless people down the block from me. As I indulge in Food Network, *Top Chef*, *Chef's Table*, and a plethora of other well-shot food and challenge shows, many people are going to bed hungry. But all those streaming options seem to be a way to fill up the actual emotional and physical wasteland in which we are currently living.

When I was home, the family and I decided to watch the documentary *13th*. A documentary, directed by Ava DuVernay, which teaches us what the American education system definitely didn't teach me. That the Thirteenth Amendment didn't actually end slavery, contrary to popular belief. It just hid it, cloaked it behind bars, and called it prison.

I had seen it before, but I had forgotten so much of it. Partly because of how our nation's hate is so blatant, scripted, and designed. From politicians and the media who all turned civil rights activists into criminals and threats to the transformation of the KKK into legal segregation and Jim Crow. The war on drugs. How prosecutors (99 percent of them being white) are the ones who sentence people to incarceration—not the judge. This is just a handful of it.

I watched that film, and I felt betrayed by my government. I couldn't help but ask, everything I have comes from that?

This led to me trying to get my father to admit he was racist.

"Admit it, racism is in our history, in our blood. It's especially in our Dominican blood." I needed him to admit it because I didn't want to be alone in my disbelief and anger.

"I'm not racist," he said.

"Everyone's a little racist," I told him, accidently quoting the *Avenue Q* song, which is a terrible illustration of what racism is and makes it seem so innocuous that we can smile about it in a Broadway musical filled with singing puppets.

I tried to explain, "It's almost impossible to escape."

He fought me with every ounce of his strength. "Bullshit," like I was challenging that he was a good person.

I told him: "Pops, you can be racist and still be a good person, I'm sure Ted Bundy washed dishes."

But he wouldn't relent. We were yelling at each other, my mom and sister just watching helplessly. Why wouldn't he admit it? Was this another example of how BIPOC can internalize racism so that they might perpetuate it and also be wounded by it simultaneously?

Eventually, I backed off, in a way I never would've with a stranger or a friend. I let him have his truth. Maybe it was out of respect, an understanding of what he sacrificed, how he's done so much for me. It's my pops for Christ's sake.

Race is not a comfortable conversation for any of us. It's not easy to take accountability, but we must all be honest about how we got here so that we can imagine a new way.

And yet, I truly believe that we are closer now to some sort of lasting change than we ever have been. I believe that something's happening. I feel like more people get it. I feel like more people understand it.

Sure, that can seem wildly optimistic in a climate that has kids locked in cages, an Artic temperature above 90 degrees, mass shootings, loneliness, parents taken from their children, a world with 550,000 homeless people in the United States, a world where we shoot $70,000 missiles from $28 million drones, flying at a cost of $3,624 an hour to kill people living on less than a dollar a day.

I'm aware of all this. The chaos of these times has frozen me from action and given me many a panic attack and sleepless night. Causing me and my actions to feel tiny and insignificant, and yet I still have hope.

Hope because of a story I read about Bernie Glassman, the founder of Zen Peacemakers. Bernie Glassman was a badass. He is known as a pioneer of social enterprise. Bernie started Greyston Bakery in Yonkers in the 1980s, even though he didn't know shit about baking. Not a damn thing. He started it because he saw that there were homeless people who needed jobs, and he liked cheesecake.

So, he starts this bakery, and he hires people who are homeless, and the bakery makes really good money. Enough money that they start buying real estate around the bakery to house the employees. Eventually, from there, they create a community that has child care, healthcare, community gardens, education, and now, even after his death, they are serving more than two thousand people a year.

Bernie was asked, "Will you really solve homelessness with just this bakery?"

He said, "Yes." He said, "Choose battles that are small enough to win and big enough to matter."

Okay. What battle do I choose, when there is so much to choose from? What battle do I choose in a country that often doesn't value me, my heart, my art, my sweat, my body, and my voice?

This is when I begin to freeze up again. I think: "If I speak, what's the point, nothing changes. My words aren't heard or welcomed."

But shit, if I'm silent, guess what? Nothing changes.

And then I stop, I breathe, and I think about Bernie and the bakery. I think about how he started a bakery without knowing anything about baking. How he took action with the intention of helping someone other than himself, something small enough that he could win and large enough that mattered.

The capacity to care for one another and to care for the planet seems to have something to do with simultaneously recognizing both our oneness, as well as what makes us specific, unique, and worth caring for. The capacity to deeply see something that we take for granted or that is invisible to us impacts our capacity for conservation and humanity. In many ways, the inability of the human race to value our planet or Brownness is detrimental not just to people of color, but to all of us.

I believe what is destroying our world is this persistent notion that we are independent of it, that we are separate from our neighbors, our trees, our air, and our blocks, that our actions don't matter in his or her life out there separate from us, that we are immune to what we do to them. It is this separation that allows someone to kneel on someone's neck for eight minutes and forty-six seconds, to shoot someone in the back nine times at point blank, and to open fire on an innocent woman who was restfully sleeping in her bed. Tiny universe—it's all connected—within each action is every action and your relationship to all things. Every inch of your life holds all of your life. Every inch of this place we call earth holds all of it and has been there for all of it. It holds the pain, grief, regret, hangovers, joy, warmth, hunger, cooking, baking, sex, potty breaks, anger, despair, pride, creativity, success, goodbyes, and beginnings, all of it.

When I think about this, that all my actions are reflective of all my other actions and my relationship to all things, I think about this poem by the late Buddhist teacher Michael Stone:

> You are not a part of nature,
> Nature is a part of you.
> Treat nature as you would your lungs or kidneys.

Which begs me to ask the question: How *do* I treat my lungs or kidneys? How do I treat myself? How do I treat others? How do I care for myself? How do I treat my community? My delivery people? My teachers? My friends? My barista? The insects that sneak into my home? How do I treat them?

Because really, it all comes down to small choices, to small actions.

Your action might be to write a really good poem. Someone's might be to tie themselves to a tree. Someone else might help someone vote, or dance in a park like no one is watching, or use breastfeeding in public as their practice. Regardless of the outcome, I imagine there is activism you are already doing that you haven't even recognized as activism. You don't have to start a business or nonprofit to make this happen.

The morning after watching the documentary *13th* and fighting with my father about our inherent racism, my mother pulled me aside and told me: "Last night your father cried in my arms like he hadn't in a lifetime. He cried and apologized for bringing his kids into this world with so much hate."

I have never seen that side of my father ever. He doesn't know my mother shared this with me (he will now). Actions can soften even the hardest stone.

Really what we're doing here is healing. Coming close to what we have avoided. Maybe letting go of preconceptions, projections, and delusions. Trusting our voice and that what we do makes a difference, how we move, how we breathe, how we speak, how we listen. We can continue to live in this disconnected way, filled with toxic patterns, or we can heal.

I love the way the French West Indian psychiatrist and political philosopher Frantz Fanon says it simply, "What matters is not to know the world but to change it."

The world that we're trying to build already exists. It just doesn't exist for everyone. It's hard to think of a world with equality, regenerative equity, sustainability, and equal rights. It's hard to imagine that this hate that is ingrained in us will ever be cleansed on a cellular level. But we have to imagine it. As the poet Clint Smith tells his future son so perfectly: "This world is a social construction; it can be reconstructed. This world was built; it can be rebuilt. Use everything that you accrue to reimagine the world."

This reimagining has begun even at the policy level: Certain states have defunded the police, police chiefs are resigning, cops are being prosecuted and convicted. Old white men who ran organizations for twenty years are stepping down. In Vermont, a list was publicly released with Black people's names and Venmo accounts so that people could send them reparations— and they did!

With all that said, it's complicated and filled with layers, but do not for one moment think you cannot change what exists. Do not believe that you can't be pessimistic and optimistic all at the same time.

The psychological term for it is cognitive dissonance. The holding of two opposing ideas in the mind at the same time. We can wish kindness for all beings and simultaneously wish the person who just cut us off in traffic is late to wherever they are going. A situation can seem hopeless, and yet we can still have hope.

Do your individual actions while also making room to remember they are public actions. This separation and degradation of people and planet is a public health problem. Public. An "all of ours" issue. We all matter, or none of us do.

Is it possible to live in a world where we all have nice things?

When the Amazon Rainforest was burning, there were all these Kickstarters and GoFundMes to help stop the fires, yes, the Amazon Rainforest needed a GoFundMe to go viral in order not to burn.

Also, donating often feels like a form of virtue signaling, a way of saying, "Look at me, I donated, I'm a good person who cares." It's like donating to Black Lives Matters organizations but not stepping up when the white people in the office keep being promoted over women and non-straight or non-white employees.

All that to say, it cost twice as much to make *The Emoji Movie* than what we donated to the rainforest.

I recall seeing an exhibit about the water stewards in Indigenous communities, and something one woman said in particular stayed with me: Essentially, she noted the power of fighting for something not from a place of anger or desperation, or wanting to do the right thing, but from deep love for our human potential and our future loved ones. She talked about caring for things versus fixing them. How a simple sense of caring has profound effects. Caring allows us to get in front of the issues before we have to fix them.

An elementary example: When I feel like throwing some trash on the floor, I wonder, would I throw this trash on top of someone's head who I cared about? Or in my neighborhood, where there is a surprising amount of stray landmines (aka dog shit), I wonder, would I let my dog shit on my mother's feet? (Some of us would, I get that.)

That trash might affect someone walking on that block or an animal might eat said trash—or as Robert Bellah says in his book *Habits of the Heart*, "We have to treat others as part of who we are, rather than as a 'them' with whom we are in constant competition." It's not only caring for the beings and life forces who are present with us currently but also beings of the future, because we are ALL going to be someone's ancestors. That is inevitable. So, what kind of ancestor am I shaping up to be?

Fuck, will I even be so lucky as to be an ancestor? It's a conversation that Miriam, my current partner, and I have: "Do we really want to bring children into a world that's just getting hotter, a world with finite resources? Lack of fresh water. Is that fair for our child?"

My partner and I have this talk all the time. I think we both want kids, but we are both afraid and aware of the climate in crisis.

I do think it is wrong to assume that I am only an ancestor if I am passing on my DNA. If I benefit in this life, from any form of basic infrastructure or great invention, clean water, a highway, electricity, then I know someone made that with me in mind—they weren't my parent or blood relative, but they did have me in mind. Being a good ancestor is the ability to keep others in mind. Care for it before you have to fix it.

Just the other day I was on a walk with my buddy, and we walked by this older gentleman, probably in his early seventies. He was watering his very green and pristine lawn (mind you, this is Los Angeles), and I said, "Wow, that's a super green lawn."

"Thank you," he replied.

He hadn't picked up on any of my sarcasm. I clarified: "You know we're in a drought, right? We live in LA, we live in a desert. You know it doesn't rain here? You know how water is a finite resource?"

"Fuck do I care. I'm gonna die soon enough. Get outta here and leave me alone."

I left him alone.

Because I don't know the answer, and we can yell at each other until we are blue in the face. I don't have a lawn to water, but I do own a shit ton of house plants that I water every Sunday. I don't save the water I use from washing the dishes and use it to flush the toilet, because I don't think I could handle a toilet full of unflushed shit waiting for me to do the dishes.

This piece is not about solutions, answers, quick fixes, or injectable optimism. Sometimes, I can't even imagine where to begin, or what to do next, or what to do at all. It can feel like so much suffering and devastation that it can take away my joy, and

I look away, I turn off the news, and (maybe) I hope someone other than me fixes it soon so I don't have to.

It's called the "bystander effect." Growing up as a kid in New York, you heard about this all the time. Someone falls down from the platform, and everyone just watches, assuming someone else will do something . . . And so we all wait . . . Worried, anxious, hoping someone will do something, because if no one is moved to do something, the person dies, and that would suck. Someone dies because no one else in the train station was moved to do anything. Everyone was waiting for someone else to show up and do something. Who will make that gesture? Who will be moved?

I can't save nature, but I do like the way Joanna Macy states it in her book *World as Lover World as Self*, "Nature saves us."

I think in order to be moved, we need to see climate change as less of an intellectual issue and more of a lived one. We have to feel the devastation on a personal level, focusing less on the solution, and attempting to actually feel the crisis of our time. It is painful, toxic, and hard to look at. It's hard, but it's also vital.

I don't want this to become just another issue we disengage from. Another thing we tweet about for a month, donate to, go on a couple marches about, share some posts about, and then slowly lose interest in. I've seen society do this time and time again. I know one of the heads of White People 4 Black Lives, and she said that when the George Floyd protests began they saw their in-person meet-ups go from ten people to a thousand overnight. Their email list grew from 10K to 100K. Now, as the dust has settled (even though it really hasn't), their numbers and donations keep dwindling. Less and less interest.

Because humans have an incredible ability to get used to anything as long as it is consistent—good or bad, we can get used to anything. As the days get hotter and the icecaps keep melting, as the climate's instability and volatility become more and more consistent, as the institutions fail us again and again, it is no longer special or extraordinary but just another thing.

Stalin, a dictator who murdered millions, knew the power of making people numb to atrocities. He said, "One death is a tragedy; one million is a statistic." How do we feel the one and not become numb to the millions?

The terrorist attacks of September 11 killed close to three thousand people, and the 9/11 Memorial Museum in Lower Manhattan is one of the most-visited in the United States. Meanwhile, diarrhea, an easily treatable condition, kills close to 2,200 people every day. There is no all-out Global War on Diarrhea, no museum.

The memorialization of 9/11 uses the deaths of the people from the Twin Towers to drive home a nationalistic rhetoric that is essentially in support of the myth of American power, exceptionalism, and resilience. I am emotionally manipulated to see certain tragedies as more important than others when they feed into the myth that is perpetuated to support existing power structures.

We are often unconsciously manipulated by forces that we cannot and do not see to conform to a hierarchy of importance—capitalism and the "growth at all costs" mentality trumps the fact that diarrhea kills 2,200 people a day.

I say this as someone who is fully indoctrinated into this way of thinking. I invest regularly in the stock market—a "growth at all cost" market, a market that exists only to keep growing and growing and growing. Which is to say, society must keep taking, taking, taking, and abusing, abusing, abusing so that we can keep the market growing, growing, growing.

Taking and abusing is part of the institution of capitalism, which is essentially incompatible with the doctrine of conservation and sustainability.

This gospel of more, more, more, more, this dependency on growth, growth, growth. Exponential growth inside a finite system will lead to collapse. It's only natural.

Maybe we should look to the news, it should guide us to the truths of our planet on a more consistent basis, it should remind us that this is a tragedy and not just a statistic, but of course it isn't that easy. My journalist friend, who shall remain nameless, told me that one of her contacts at CNN told her: "News channels have the numbers and research to prove that talking about climate change makes people sad. It's too depressing, they stop reading, or they turn off the TV. We can't afford people turning off the TV."

Even CNN can't afford the truth.

The truth is, I'm no saint, it isn't just the planet I grieve for, it's myself. It's my life. It's my air-conditioning bill as it gets hotter every year. It's me wondering if I don't like to waste food because I want to cut back on waste or because I'm another inner-city kid who needed to make every meal count. It's me not wanting to live in some sort of dried-up desert like in *The Book of Eli* or some devasted Waterworld (I actually think I would be a pretty good Kevin Costner–type antihero if it came down to that—but I don't want that). It's my own fear, because the trees will come again, our planet will survive (no matter how much we take from it), it is we who won't survive.

In *The Book of Delights*, Ross Gay describes joy as "entering and joining with the terrible." Choosing to enter and choosing to join with the terrible, not just an entering and joining with the pleasant stuff but the ability to be present with it all.

And we (each and every one of us) all experience it ALL: pain, sorrow, hurt, boredom, joy, worry, doubt, confusion, and the great inevitable death, of ourselves and of our loved ones. That is what binds us.

What if we all took a page out of Ross Gay's book and consciously acknowledged and entered that terribleness together, could we then face the catastrophes and devastations of our world without needing to look away? Could facing our justifications and dismissal of hundreds of years of dehumanizing "others" reveal in us other issues that need facing (we got a lot of stuff to face)? How do we do this? First we have to be brave enough to not turn off the sad stuff. Brave enough to not look away. Brave enough to know that we can't dehumanize others without dehumanizing ourselves. Brave enough to know it's all connected. We have to get intimate with the current catastrophe we are all living in. We have to feel the grief and pain of it, we have to enter.

If cops wear body cameras to share acts of discrimination and injustice, so that we can see, feel, and awaken to the pain of that ignorance, should trees? Would we march for a viral tree cutting?

This planet provides all our food, clothing, shelter, and material wealth, and she doesn't care about race or gender, she shows complete equality and generosity toward all. She's trying to heal you, let it happen. Or as Joanna Macy, an environmental activist, author, scholar of Buddhism, systems theorist, and ecologist (longest business card ever) puts it: "As we work to heal the Earth, the Earth heals us. No need to wait."

This is why I have started taking my weekly talk therapy sessions on the phone: as I walk around my block, and talk and vent, and clear my mind, I also collect trash.

This action goes far beyond the climate. As I walk and collect trash, I imagine others, the planet, my future, our children's future (if we choose to have them, if we *get* to have them). As my mind gets clearer from the therapy and my block gets a little clearer from the trash removal, I imagine equality, healing, and restoration, large and small for all. Envisioning what recovery, loving, and nurturing this planet and one another looks like in a new way, because it isn't this.

Then I can begin to walk in that direction.

And I'm a fast walker, y'all. Really, not just because I am a New Yorker, I just always have somewhere to be. Recently, in Prospect Park, I watched a mother hold her child's hand as she walked so slowly along a curb. One foot in front of the other. So damn slow. I thought, will I ever be able to walk that slow? I hope so. I hope this is me walking slowly, without a destination, walking not to get somewhere or fix something but rather to care, to be present, to be aware of what is happening, one foot in front of the other. Nothing more, nothing less. If knocked down and frozen with overwhelm and grief, I begin again, I persist, I enter into the terribleness again. Because, this is my home, and these are my people, and I'm in it for the long haul. Through all the madness, the seesaw, ups and downs of the world, health, government, policies, society, life, and love I persist, because in the long run it is perseverance, my ability to be present with it all, and persistence that shapes the future and shapes the now.

One foot in front of the other. Like the slow growth Redwoods that have been here since the beginning of time. One moment at a time. One foot and then another.

> "As we work to heal the Earth, the Earth heals us.
> No need to wait."

—JOANNA MACY,

WORLD AS LOVER, WORLD AS SELF

Alchemy of Brownness

"The thing America fears most is the
Browning of America."

—RICHARD RODRIGUEZ

People often ask me if I'm Middle Eastern. I say, "Nope,
I'm Latin."

They say: "Oh, cool, cool, cool. Where you from?"

"New York," I say.

"Oh, you're Puerto Rican," they respond with confidence.

"Nope, Dominican."

"Oh. That's cool. I know some Dominicans."

"Wow. That's cool. I know some white people," I say. "So,
we're even."

In the Dominican Republic I'm everything from white to *prieto* to *cocolo*, referring to my non-Hispanic African descendants, to *mulatto*, referring to my mixed African and European ancestry. When someone isn't sure about me, they say, *Mira detrás de las orejas,* or look behind the ears, as if that is where the Blackness is hiding. In Colombia, I am *trigueño*—light Brown or coffee-colored, or possibly mestizo—of mixed race, having Spanish and Indigenous descent. In many Spanish speaking places, they would advise me against calling myself Afro-Latino, because if I am light-skinned enough to pass, then I should choose to pass.

In America, I am Brown. In many a cab, I am South Asian. I have been told I look like someone's Armenian, Indian, or Greek cousin more than a dozen times. In some malls where they have those Dead Sea beauty products that they sell very aggressively, I am Israeli. I've had a handful of people tell me, "I like Latins, they're lovers, not fighters." One, that's actually very historically inaccurate. Spaniards were pretty fucking vicious. And two, you don't know me.

In Hollywood, I am just enough of a mutt and a little bit of everything that they call me Ethnically Ambiguous, which means exactly what it sounds like, I look ambiguous enough that my ethnicity cannot be identified. It's a way of labeling me by not labeling me. Means for studios and advertisers I can check multiple race boxes at once, which is great for their diversity and inclusion numbers. I'll admit, I am aware of my odd privilege of being ambiguous, there is something about people not being able to know quite where I'm from, when they look at me it allows me movement. I can dance, hang, and hide in multiple spaces and circles, but also it never truly allows me a safe place to call home.

What is Brownness? The vague but large gap in the middle where things are forgotten, often don't exist, don't matter, and don't belong.

What is Brownness? A concept. An ambiguous identity that doesn't offer the same diasporic bond as being Black, yet it provides none of the power or grace that comes with navigating the world as white.

What is Brownness? *Everything* between Black and white.

What is Brownness? The global majority.

It's all just a spectrum, it all depends on who you ask, what they stand for, where you are, what you want, what they need, what you acknowledge, and when and where.

In the book *Me and White Supremacy,* Layla F. Saad writes, "You cannot challenge what you do not understand." In the spirit of challenging, with the goal of disrupting, in the spirit of understanding, I will present a little context on Brownness:

The color Brown has always played an important role in the life of America and the entire world. From Indians and their centuries-old caste system, Cubans with unspoken colorist standards, and Dominicans's self-hatred due to their connection with Haiti, Asia, and the Middle East, the conflict with Brownness and wanting to move closer to whiteness is embedded in our histories. The perpetuation of white supremacist standards is universal, from Pakistan to Panama. Monoethnic countries deal with it too.

But non-Black people of color do not easily fit into the binary boxes of Black or white. Our races, ethnicities, and heritages matter! What separates us in phenotypes unites us in birthright.

A couple of years ago, I was sitting with a friend in Mexico as she told me this story about an article she read in the *New York Times*: "Apparently, there's this new procedure where people pump glutathione—an antioxidant in plants, animals, and shit—into their veins in the hopes of lightening their skin."

I took a sip of my Victoria cerveza and wondered, "Wow, the inability to live comfortably in our own skin has come to that."

But then I confessed to her: "You know, my Dominican grand-mother used to come over and check the width of my nose? Yeah, she would ask my parents if I was really squeezing and pulling it forward. Then she would insist that I sleep with a clothespin pinched to my nose, to help keep it thin, like they do it back in el campo. Worst part about it . . . I did it."

"Yeah, I did that too," Sandy said.

I stopped for maybe half a second, nodded, received this in-formation, and continued on with my own thoughts, ignoring her statement until she stopped me. "You just bulldozed over what I said."

I stopped and took a breath, and it was in that breath that I broke. I started weeping. I explained to her through tears and snot, in the middle of a crowded café over my bowl of *caldo de res*, "I heard you, I did, but I was afraid to stop, I knew if I stopped and made room for it, if I really took this information in, I would break, and this would happen."

"It sucks," she said with confidence.

I agreed, "It does suck."

We sat there in silence, eyes watery. "Who told you to do that?" I asked.

"I don't know," she said, "There was not a particular person, maybe I just made it up."

"Made it up?"

Do we, can we, make up this feeling of disgust directed to-ward our own bodies? Is this why as a child I would cry in front of the mirror while looking at my skin, my thick hair, big ears, and my large wide nose? I would turn on the shower, close the door, and look into the vanity above the sink. I would examine myself, slowly, inch by inch. And the tears would start . . . I couldn't explain it then, other than that my body was holding shame, my skin holding a long history of needing to be loved, my skin feeling a sadness that my mind couldn't yet register.

Is it just something we inherit? Or does someone have to teach it to us? Did my friend really just make it up that she needed to spend hours in front of the mirror tucking in her lips to practice smiling white? Do we make up our self-hate? How does a little girl come to feel intuitively that this world isn't made for her, her body, her lips, her beautiful face?

I think that white supremacy is also a kind of evil alchemy, the kind that can turn someone into no one. The kind that makes you only look outside of yourself for validation from someone else. It can take a body of culture with so much to give and tell it that it has nothing to offer, that it is not worthy of love unless it is something else, saying turn your gold into metal, when really, your gold should stay exactly as is.

That night, we shared with each other things we had never told anyone before. I voiced to her secrets and stories about my self-hate and body dysmorphia that I have tried to push down and forget, the ways in which I have cut into and changed my body. The nights where I stayed awake praying to be someone else. We cried for her, for me, for all the little Brown boys and girls who somehow just intuitively feel that their bodies aren't enough. I don't think that night healed us entirely, but it certainly felt nice to be heard and to confide in each other, to know we weren't alone.

This is the alchemy of Brownness.

Because Brownness, like Blackness, contains so much nuance, color, a multitude of races, ethnicities, and nationalities. Brownness is the space in-between, or the *bardo* space as written about in Tibetan scripture, the powerful transformative space in-between from which we humans can break free from our illusions, labels, and stories, and see what really is: Something that can't be summed up into just two lines, because it is not a clean line, and it never will be.

But America (maybe humans in general) have a fixation and need to compartmentalize. We love clean lines and do not handle those in-between spaces very well. Many of us seem to struggle or have a possible inability to understand anything outside of the simple "this or that" mentality—just look at the immense struggle to understand gender fluidity.

My homie, Miranda, has been thinking about transitioning to they. It started at home and slowly leaked its way into the world. They told their father, and he got grumpy, not mad, grumpy. His brain hurt, he didn't understand it. "There aren't two of you," he said, "I just don't get it."

I smiled when they told me this. His grumpiness opened a door for me—he wasn't mad with them, he was confused. We fear what we don't know, what we can't understand. Nobody wants to be confused, and so we make the world binary and dualistic, and put things in boxes with clear labels because, admittingly, it's easier that way. As a kid, when I found my dad's label machine, I wanted to label everything. It felt powerful to be able to claim what something was; whether I named it as my property or whether I just named it—my favorite mug, my favorite cereal, my favorite cereal spoon (it's hard to label a spoon, you don't actually want to put the label on the part where you put your mouth).

It's far more difficult to expand our minds to places that we don't understand; to embrace the confusion and make room for the unknown. To see all the shades, all the nuances, and all the contradictions that go into this life. Wanting to not be left out, we grasp firmly onto the known, we stand on what we know, because we cannot sit comfortably on the things we don't.

For most people, the things we don't understand will make us grumpy. Might even scare us or make us feel unsafe. This need for safety leads to categorizing, which quickly turns into mine versus yours, us versus them, this versus that, which quickly turns to competition. We make it to where things like size, age, color, the amount of melanin in one's skin, and which parts of the body stick out most determine the course of one's life. Just look at the easily forgotten American eugenics movement (which predated and inspired the Nazi movement), which sterilized sixty-four thousand women in hopes of clearing out the "unfit" and "undesirable" from society. Society has allowed white supremacy to make choices about who counts (and who doesn't) for a very long time.

So globally, systematically, effectively, we find and create ways to make people of color identify with the body that will accept it most or the group that will allow it the most social mobility—if you're lucky, if your hair can be calmed, your skin is just light enough, your features Eurocentric enough, your presence more acceptable than threatening, then how you pass and where you fall on the color line is a choice you can maybe make on your own.

We wouldn't have a world where "passing" occurred if there were no incentives associated with "whiteness." It's all about belonging and being seen. Belonging is hardwired in us. We are tribal. Each and every one of us wants to be a part of something. We want to look across the room and know that another person has our back, we want to walk into a room and know, I am safe here. There isn't a person who isn't seeking some sort of recognition. And who do most people rich with melanin care to be seen by? The dominant and often less melanin rich other. In his book *Black Skin, White Masks,* Frantz Fanon writes:

> Man is human only to the extent to which he tries to impose himself on another man in order to be recognized by him. As long as he has not been effectively recognized by the other, it is this other who remains the focus of his actions. His human worth and reality depend on this other and on his recognition by the other. It is in this other that the meaning of his life is condensed.

In my family there is a story of legend, my parents have told it to me a million times, it's about the night my pops first found out my mother was pregnant. It was a summer night in 1984, my mom and Pops had been hanging with some friends and were headed home. It was 3 a.m. and they were waiting for the 7 train in Jackson Heights, Queens, Roosevelt station. It was empty, it was quiet.

They're just sitting there in silence, when my twenty-year-old mom breaks the silence by telling my twenty-three-year-old pops that she's pregnant. With my older sister, their first kid.

This was a surprise.

My mom was an immigrant, an outsider, and Pops was first generation. This was new territory for both of them.

That information hung in the air for a hot minute . . . My mom was just waiting for some sort of reaction, when my pops finally asked her: "Okay. Well, what do you want, Nena?"

My mom said: "I want my kids to never have to worry about where their next meal comes from, something more than we had. Something more than a single mattress on the floor of a studio apartment. Something more than spaghetti and hotdogs for dinner."

And my pops replied: "Okay, let's do it. Let's do it."

"How?" she asked.

"I don't know . . . But we'll do it, no matter what."

This was when these two young Latinos decided that they were going to turn nothing into something—remember alchemy? My parents were the poster children for Alchemy 101—they decided to give their children everything they never had by taking what was there and making it more. My parents were my first example of the transformation that is possible when you keep taking actions and pushing forward in the right direction, and that it doesn't all have to be figured out beforehand, you just have to keep moving forward. They didn't have a game plan, and they for sure didn't have all the right pieces. They simply said, "We will do anything to make it happen." And they did.

"This was the scariest conversation we ever had in our forty-plus years together," my mom says.

They made a promise to each other. My pops said: "We will do it, whatever we have to do in order for our children to have a better life than us, we will do it. We will give them what we never had. By any means necessary."

When my mother and father were born in the '50s and '60s they didn't even have the option of being Hispanic or Latino on their birth certificates. Because it wasn't until the 1980s that the United States created the term "Hispanic" to classify *all* peoples who come from Spanish-speaking countries.

These little boxes that divide also bring some people together. In my parents' case, there is loneliness when you don't have a box, when you're between boxes. Now, my parents and I have a box that is closer to representing our Brownness yet still very far from containing its diverse complexity.

The language of identity fails us—"Hispanic," "Latino," or "Latino/a/X/e"—as if a single term could ever represent the two dozen countries of origin from which we come, the Indigenous tribes it was created to erase, and generations of peoples and cultures intermingling.

Latinos are the second largest demographic in the United States. According to the US Census Bureau, America is becoming Browner. The census report indicates that in about twenty-five years, the US population will become "majority minority." But, what does that actually mean? Are Latinos a race? An ethnicity? A culture? *Latinidad*, or whatever term you try and lock us into, means being from everywhere, and yet I must find my box, I must find where I belong.

It's always more complex. The reality is also that "whiteness" as a label is also a construct, and these categories we see as being monolithic are much more elastic (and often defined by those in power) than we think.

W. E. B. Du Bois said that the problem of his time was the problem of the color line—a line of societal and/or legal barriers that segregated Black people from white people. If we're being honest, which is hard for some of us (I get it, because honesty is not always pretty or happy, and it doesn't always make you and your ancestry and your ideals, the things you stand on, seem so ideal, I get it), if we're being honest, that line of separation was drawn fat and thick, and it's still very much here. It permeates the air with every shooting, every Fox News broadcast, every debate, every highway, every city, every march, every protest, every clan, every secret meeting, every movie, every group, every suburb, everything you love, there is still that one line. Still here, and still as bold as ever.

I don't think we are very close to erasing this one line anytime soon. As much as I'd like that, I don't see it disappearing in my lifetime. Don't think I don't want this line to vanish, I want it by any means necessary.

For now, I take what's here, and what's here is still this *one* line, separating Blacks and whites. And me, and many of the Brown people I love, value, and respect, are stuck, floating somewhere in the middle—between Black and white, not seen, not heard, not recognized. To clarify, when I say Brownness, I am not just talking Latino, Hispanic, LatinX, etc. This goes way beyond that Latinidad spectrum . . . I am talking about any Brown-skinned person who feels stuck in the in-between, feeling like they have to pick a side, questioning whether or not they're doing Brownness right. Wondering, can't we be a little bit of all things? Wondering, as police officers continue to shoot unarmed Black men without consequences, and young white boys tote around assault rifles with ease, where does my Brownness stand, and how can my Brown body help? None of this is meant to be an easy definition of Brownness, just part and parcel of my perspective, which is bound to have limitations and holes because I'm just one person trying to not look at the sky through a straw, acting like I can see the whole thing.

Given all this, what is a Brown boy to do? Ask his mama of course!

I called her, and after telling me, "You only call me when you need something" (not 100 percent true, I'm working on it), she said, "Chris, in every challenging situation you have four options." She explained that we all have the choice to:

Exit: Leave, leave your country, leave your spouse, leave your job, leave the conflict, just leave, get up, and go.

Neglect: Do as little as possible, try to go unnoticed, try and forget what's happening, try and fill up your life with side hobbies and addictions that allow you to forget.

Persist: Sit with it. See what's happening, and persist on. Believe in things changing, believe in yourself, believe in a new tomorrow, and believe that things will get better.

Voice: Voice your concerns. Speak up and out against injustice. Speak your truth, because if you don't, who will? Tell your lover that y'all need counseling. Tell your boss that things need to change. Be a voice for the people in a corrupt government. Be a voice for the people who are voiceless. Voice is an act of leadership.

She shared: "What you choose is up to you. There is no right or wrong, just choices. What you choose depends on your level of commitment. What you choose reveals the worth of the thing itself."

My mom got mad wisdom. But I knew for me, I only had one option.

Voice. I choose Voice.

I can't deny who or what I am. And I have persisted long enough. We live in a world where people of color are constantly asked to persist, to give up parts of ourselves in order to move forward. This isn't new information but it's worth reiterating. We constantly have to swallow our pride, we constantly have to say things in ways that others will accept or understand. This alchemy of understanding, alchemy of loving one's Brownness, it's challenging, tedious, but also it's necessary work.

During a talkback, after one of my storytelling performances, a white woman raised her hand and said to the group in a combative way, "Do you also know how many shades of white there are?" Her tone was defensive, carrying a fear as if she was about to be erased.

I said: "For sure. Absolutely lady. Do you know how many shades of everything there are? It's not that simple. The Inuit have fifty different words for snow. It's corny, I know. But how can we expect to talk about race, pain, humanness, colonization, systematic oppression, desire, skin, trauma, Eurocentric beauty standards, slavery, and inequality with just two words, with just two colors?"

My favorite fact about the Inuit is that *Inuit* means "human." They never wanted to forget the fact that they are human. In being human, there is a *lot* to consider, it's never so simple as Black and white, where your ancestors are from, and the one word for snow.

I don't believe the solution is in erasing the line, or pretending it isn't there, like the woman who said to me, "I don't see color, people aren't white, paper is white, people are pink." Colors and hues are what make us. Cultural heritage is not and never will be a clean line, and because of this I think we all need our own lines and then a thousand more lines. Followed by a thousand more. Probably even a thousand more after that. Identifying and seeing more shades, more colors, more shadows, more. If there are fifty ways to lose your lover, and the Inuit have fifty words for snow, then I need at least fifty pronouns, labels, shades, and words that contain the universe and all its nuances alive inside of me—at least fifty.

We have to burn down classifications about what is worth it, who fits, and who doesn't. By identifying and seeing more colors, more shadows, more nuances, more cultures, more people, more flavors, more than we can even imagine, more, more, more. By identifying more, we can finally begin to see ourselves, now we don't just enter a conversation, we aren't simply invited to the table, we dismantle it and build a new one together.

My shade as a cisgendered, Dominican, Afro-Latino, Colombian New Yorker, with time spent in Miami, LA, Budapest, Belgrade, with a history of displacement, violence, love, sex, fear, fake-it-till-you-make-it, ancestral trauma, bad Spanish, color, code-switching, Hollywood, salsa (the dance and the food), and white-washing is unique.

As is yours. Your shade, your story, your hue, your history, your pain, your blood, your love, your desire, your ancestry, all of you. Let it all in, celebrate it, own it. There is incredible power when we make the great shift from simply believing someone else's story to the journey of celebrating our own.

If you are reading this, then there is a piece of you that knows the two-sided monster simply known as "Black and white" hasn't gotten us very far. In fact, at times it feels like it has gotten us nowhere. A piece of you is striving for connection, for beauty, for calm. A piece of you is ready for your voice and your truth in a world where on every corner, there is fear, confusion, ugliness, acts of terror, inequality, violence, and hate. This goes beyond your color, pronoun, beyond your label machine and your "I must understand" box.

Again, I choose voice. I choose voice for the young, beautiful Brown girls and boys who don't see themselves and who think they don't have a place in all this. I choose voice, the vital necessity of being identified, seen, and heard; to be in the conversation. I choose voice for those who are unaware of the courage and audacity it takes to be a person of color in this world, the courage to walk out into the world and declare: "I am worth it, I will be seen, I matter. I am the other body in the room. I am in the conversation. I am here."

My story is a simple one, even though it often feels radical—my story is about choosing to love my Brownness. It's about thriving in a world not made for me, because Brownness taking up space should not be a radical act.

As I've said, Brown is not just the story of "Woe is me," it's about "Yeah is us!" Because Brown is in the relentless conversation of white and Black, the conversation of who is and who isn't worth it. Because we are in it, we have to be in it. What we currently have, this checkerboard of Black versus white, isn't working, it isn't cutting it. It's time for a new game with new pieces and new colors—starting with the many, many, many shades, ideas, and people that Brownness embraces.

A Final Note

To all my beautiful Brown people, for too long there has existed a whole spectrum of not belonging, now we take that whole field of color between Black and white and make it our spectrum of belonging as well. Yes, sometimes we fall within the cracks, and sometimes we will still wonder where we belong, but we can always remind ourselves: Here. I belong here. Right here. Always here. Without all the shapeshifting and pretending. Here, we are safe to be ourselves, here, we are safe to feel our grief and our hope. Here, we can begin to alchemize and embody self-love, liberation, and justice, not in a whoo-hoo hippie social media way but an actual we are worthy of self-love and waking up and taking up space and going to bed in peace kind of way. In an *I don't care what you think* kind of way. This new alchemy, this transformation of self-hate into self-love, can't happen in a vacuum, and it is much easier said than done. It takes work, community, positive reinforcement, reminders, and sometimes a little help.

And just because there is a Brown body in the room does not mean we cannot perpetuate harmful systems of power as well, or that we are not capable of exclusion. I want us to think more deeply about how we are using our unique privilege (gained from being able to sometimes play both sides). Are we committed to antiracist work in all the spaces, no matter how uncomfortable it may make us?

The book of who we are is not a fixed text, it is flowing, it is fluid, it is expansive, it is often Brown. We are shaping it, right here, right now.

Thank you for taking this journey with me.

Much love and many blessings.

About the Author

CHRISTOPHER RIVAS is an actor, author, podcaster, and storyteller best known for his onscreen work on the Fox series *Call Me Kat*. In addition, he hosts two podcasts on SiriusXM's Stitcher: *Rubirosa*, a limited series about the life of Porfirio Rubirosa, and the weekly show *Brown Enough*. He is a PhD candidate in expressive arts for global health and peacebuilding at The European Graduate School and a Rothschild social impact fellow. Rivas resides in Los Angeles.